Daily Essentials

Volume 1

Principles for Life
Management

BOBBY BOGARD

ISBN: 978-1-7350642-2-2

DEDICATION

I don't believe the human story can be told without relational interactions, seasonal transitions, or unplanned experiences. Daily Essentials is written from those three paradigms. Therefore, it is imperative that I dedicate this book to the Beautiful Rose of Texas, my wife of forty-five years as of this writing. She has traveled with me through traumatic events, weathered numerous family & friend dilemmas, and supported me in every endeavor and challenge I brought into our lives. The stories, illustrations, insights, perspectives and even presuppositions shared in this book, all emerge from the seasons, encounters, and surprises we survived. I hope you learn something from us. I trust something in this book will give you the courage to dream big, to live without fear, and to seize each day's possibilities.

I also dedicate this book to you... the reader. Your life matters. Your story is still in process. Your past has been lived but, "The Best is Yet To Be!" Take life a day at a time and enjoy the journey.

Contents

Daily Essentials

Part One
Personal Development

Daily Essential One - FILL THE ROOM

When you enter a room for the first time what catches your attention? My wife is an interior designer and when she enters a room for the first time she is looking at color schemes, room layouts, and decor. I walk into the same room, and I'm looking for the most comfortable seating in proximity to the television. When I enter a business for the first time, I look at the room from a proficiency standpoint. How are customers being served? What is the process for delivering the product in a timely manner? Is it easy to find what I am looking for, and if I need a question answered can the staff answer it? Think about when you enter a friend's house for the first time as their guest. You enter their home, and you are observing how they fill their rooms. You notice family portraits, arrangement of furniture, and styles of window dressings. You will formulate certain opinions and walk away with a certain point of view simply by how they fill their room. You may have been in a communications class and taught how to read the room. It's what helps you connect with your audience. The room is significant, and what it is filled with is telling.

Have you ever considered the room of your heart and soul? Have you ever paused to think about how influential it is? I'm talking about the room that houses the core of our identity. The place where the true self lives. It's the room where we invite family, friends, and even outsiders to when we want to share our experiences. The place we open when we want to help others glean from our story. We welcome people in when we know the room is filled with life and peace. It's also the room we refuse to open at times because it is filled with hurts, wounds, and unforgiveness. We shut the door tight because opening it would expose our motives, weaknesses, and sins. How we fill this room will determine the quality of life that we live with others. What activity happens in this room will impact the influence that we ultimately carry. The scriptures teach us that out of this room emerge all the issues of our lives. The

Bible encourages us to put a guard over it so that what we fill it with will be life giving to ourselves and others. When people enter our room, something will catch their attention. They will observe the fixtures, the ambiance, the activity, the pictures, and they will walk away with life or death simply by how we fill the room.

DAILY ESSENTIALS

HERE IS MY QUESTION: What is the condition of your room (heart)?

_____

_____

_____

_____

_____

_____

_____

_____

HERE IS MY CHALLENGE: Ask yourself, "How can I remodel this room and make it better?"

_____

_____

_____

_____

_____

_____

_____

_____

Daily Essential Two - LIVING BEYOND THE EXTREMES

When I was young, my mom had to flee some very difficult circumstances. We packed as much as we could in a few suitcases and boarded a train to California. We ended up in Beverly Hills just down the street from several movie stars. The home was a mansion with a large pool in the backyard. The oldest son of this family lived in the pool house which was larger than the home we left in Texas. I thought we were in paradise. Since that experience years ago, I have had the privilege of serving in third world countries. It is overwhelming to see such impoverished and suffering people. They have to ration water, electrical power outages happen regularly, and food is scarce at times. Children play in the streets with sticks, or other objects of nature they can use to make a game. There is a stark contrast between wealth and poverty, but those are the extremes.

The Apostle Paul makes an interesting observation about provisions. He said, "I know how to live on almost nothing or with everything. I have learned the secret of living in every situation, whether it is with a full stomach or empty, with plenty or little." Learning the secret of living beyond the extremes brings great contentment into our lives. Contentment seems to be a rare commodity in today's culture. Needy people tend to be very impatient and dissatisfied. They struggle with patience. They complain. They seek instant gratification. Simultaneously there are those with abundance. They contend with their own attitudes. These can range from pride and arrogance to a lack of compassion toward those in need. These individuals may struggle with greed and envy. Needless to say, poverty or abundance have their own particular battles. Paul implies that both extremes need to discover the secret of living in contentment.

PRINCIPLES FOR LIFE MANAGEMENT

Living beyond the extremes is coming to a place where we manage our impatience or our attitudes. It's the art of being content and fulfilled no matter the status of our financial position. It's recognizing the power of thankfulness and the force of generosity. Contentment is a sweet spot of life that many fail to discover.

DAILY ESSENTIALS

HERE IS MY QUESTION: On a scale of 1 to 10, how would you rank your contentment?
(1=poor; 10=excellent)

HERE IS MY CHALLENGE: Move up the scale.

PRINCIPLES FOR LIFE MANAGEMENT

Daily Essential Three - LIVE, LEAD, LEARN

LIVE IN THE MOMENT! Recently the Beautiful Rose of Texas (my wife) and I were taking a Sunday afternoon drive. I was taking in all the beauty of Michigan and noticed Rose on her cell phone. I said, "Babe you're missing the moment!" If we are not careful that is how we live our lives.... distracted. We miss opportunities, we miss relationships, we miss the splendor of creation, and we miss the precious moment we can never recover. Live in the moment!

LEAD YOURSELF TO CHANGE! Do you remember life before and after marriage? Can you recall how you felt when you bought your first car? How was the first day you went to work? All of these events involved adjustments and brought different experiences into our lives. Change is a critical part of life. Transitions are necessary for progress. Growth requires change. Most of us resist change because of the work or the loss that it requires. The reality is that change is coming like it or not. We are going to get older. Our kids will leave the house (hopefully)! The car will need to be replaced. Culture will shift and trends will vary. These things will impact our budgets, our emotions, our physical well being, and much more. Rather than reinforce and entrench ourselves in a posture of resistance to transformation, we should lead ourselves to the right modifications. Get ahead of the game and lead yourself to change.

LEARN ALL YOU CAN WHILE YOU CAN! This morning I replayed a video of my oldest grandson trying to sing "Old McDonald had a farm!" He must have been about two-and-a-half years old. He got the words mixed up and he didn't get the tune quite right, but he was learning. Learning is what opens up new horizons. We peer into things that we never imagined. We secure information that brings new understanding. We progress when we learn. We gain insights into others, and how

7

they experience life. Then we are able to build relational bridges that lead to reconciliation. Learning can only occur if we pursue it. We have to pick up a book. We have to enter into a conversation. We have to seek out education and pay the tuition. We have to posture ourselves for learning. We have to be teachable. We have to be vulnerable. We have to value the opportunity to learn. Learning is necessary for success. Learn all you can while you can!

DAILY ESSENTIALS

HERE IS MY QUESTION: Where are you falling behind?

_____

_____

_____

_____

_____

_____

_____

_____

HERE IS MY CHALLENGE: Live! Lead! Learn!

_____

_____

_____

_____

_____

_____

_____

_____

_____

Daily Essential Four - RESERVED FOR...

Have you ever been in a hurry to park your car only to find a sign the says "Reserved For...?" The spot might be for Expectant Mothers, Employee of the Month, or someone who is handicapped. The point is the spot is designated for someone besides you, so you have to find another place to park. It doesn't matter how much time you have, how busy you are, or how close you want to park to the establishment you are patronizing, you cannot park there. It is reserved. You park on the next row, get out of your car, and head into the facilities. Then, some self-absorbed person parks in a "reserved" spot and you know he is not pregnant, definitely not an employee, nor is he handicapped. You want to say something but refrain.

I wonder how many people park themselves in our lives. They come unannounced into our world to dump their problems, to impose on our time, or ask for our resources. They are in a hurry to get their need met and move on to their next item of business. They have no self-awareness. They ignore the "reserved sign" and barge right into our space. We want to say something but restrain ourselves. So, we let them leave their brokenness in our hearts, we allow them to roll over our emotions, we permit them to steal our time, and we give them aid. Even well-meaning family, friends, and co-workers can be guilty of parking in the spots reserved for our rest, our immediate family, and our well-being.

Here are some pointers to protect our space. We need to make sure our space is clearly marked with signage (communication) that explains its purpose; "Downtime Needed," "Family Time," "Sabbatical." Next we should ticket those who violate the space; for example... "I will make an exception this time, but you will need to make an appointment in the future." If they continue to park there, you will need to tow their car; remove all access until they get the message. Lastly, be sure you park there regularly. When we fail to use our space, then it is assumed that the space is available.

DAILY ESSENTIALS

HERE IS MY QUESTION: Do you have some reserved spots in your life for your well-being?

_____

_____

_____

_____

_____

_____

_____

_____

_____

HERE IS MY CHALLENGE: Make sure you have them, use them, and protect them.

_____

_____

_____

_____

_____

_____

_____

_____

PRINCIPLES FOR LIFE MANAGEMENT

Daily Essential Five - BAKE IT OR FRY IT?

Have you ever been to a state fair and run across some of the most outlandish things that people fry? Fried butter, fried Oreos, fried beer, fried pickles, fried Krispy Kreme donuts, fried pigs ears, fried bubblegum, fried jelly beans, fried ice cream, cheeseburgers, fried Kool Aid, and the list goes on and on. You almost have a heart attack just reading the list. I have to admit there are some fried foods that are very appealing to me; chicken fried steak, fried chicken, fried okra (not a personal favorite but a lot of my family like it), French fries and fried catfish with some fried hush puppies! Hmmm GOOD! While fried foods can be tasty, crunchy, and satisfy in the moment, they tend to sit heavy on the stomach and make you want to take a nap. Contrast that with baked foods; baked salmon, baked chicken, baked potatoes, baked casserole, baked vegetables, and baked desserts. These dishes seem to take longer to cook, they are healthier on the digestive system, and they have less calories than fried foods. Every day we make choices about our food intake. We pay the price or reap the rewards of those regular dietary choices. Our intake of food determines our energy level, longevity of life, and physical stamina.

We also make choices daily about what feeds our souls. What we consume emotionally, intellectually, and spiritually have a great impact upon the quality of life we live. Just like we make food choices, we make choices regarding our friends, our media consumption, the values we adhere to, and the sources of our spirituality. We reap the rewards or the consequences of those decisions. The scriptures invite us to taste and see that the Lord is good, and to know that His loving kindness and tender mercies are new every day. Joshua challenged the nation of Israel to choose between life and death when they entered the promised land.

DAILY ESSENTIALS

The truth is we choose between life and death every day. Just like there are some crazy fried foods that we would never eat on a regular basis, there are some crazy philosophies and beliefs we would never embrace. However, there are some fried foods that are a temptation. We know we shouldn't make them a steady diet, but it's easy to fall into "just this once" mindset. Once we do, then it's easier to blow off the disciplines of healthy eating. The same holds true for the regimen of our spiritual, emotional, and intellectual well being. The "one time" attitude can lead to the second, the third, and ultimately to the habit of poor choices. Before we realize it, we are unhealthy, discouraged with our life, and ready to concede to the enslavement that follows. The alternative is to structure our lifestyle within the perimeters of healthy and life giving environments that enhance our relationships, our spiritual development, and our growth as individuals.

Every day is a choice. Will we bake it or will we fry it?

DAILY ESSENTIALS

HERE IS MY QUESTION: Are you frying or baking today?

_____

_____

_____

_____

_____

_____

_____

_____

HERE IS MY CHALLENGE: Start your day by reflecting on God's Promises, His Word, and His Kindness. Now seize the day by choosing life!

_____

_____

_____

_____

_____

_____

_____

_____

_____

Daily Essential Six - IN IT FOR THE LONG HAUL

Have you ever been on a trip with your family, and it seems like you'll never arrive at your destination? You drive for hours and you're still hundreds of miles away. Inevitably someone asks, "How much farther?" You wish you could be teleported. It doesn't matter how much longer it will take, how tired you are, or how many more pit stops will be needed, you are determined to get there. When you started the trip you were in it for the long haul!

I have been in ministry for over forty-five years. I would say that I have been in it for the long haul. There were times I wondered if I would make it, times when we had no money, times when we were betrayed by people close to us, times when we had to uproot our family and move across the country, and times when we were discouraged with the outcomes of our efforts. The long haul is not for the faint of heart. The long haul requires grit. However, there are some keys we can learn from our road trip analogy that will help us arrive at our intended destination.

The first and most important is never try to drive the long haul alone. It can be done, but it is dangerous. I always loved that I could take a break for a couple of hours and let the Beautiful Rose of Texas take the wheel. When you don't travel alone, there is someone on board who has your back. Secondly, make it a rule that no one is allowed to ask, "How much longer?" The Bible says that hope that is deferred makes the heart sick. You must enjoy the journey. Our lives are really more about the journey than they are the destination. The other day we were looking at the fall colors in our city. You miss those when you're concerned about getting somewhere faster.

Another bit of advice is to use all the resources at your disposal to make the trip comfortable. I only wish we had had iPads, game apps, videos, and earbuds when we traveled with our kids. We used road games, made the back of the vehicle a camp out, and sang songs. Lastly, take breaks. We are always at our best when we are rested. God took a break after six days work, and we should have a rhythm of life that allows us to chill. A deep breath of fresh air can go a long way! Like we mentioned, the long haul is not for the faint of heart, so make sure you have travel companions, enjoy the trip, utilize your resources, and give yourself a break once in a while.

DAILY ESSENTIALS

HERE IS MY QUESTION: What does this analogy speak to you about the journey you are on?

_____

_____

_____

_____

_____

_____

_____

_____

_____

HERE IS MY CHALLENGE: Make your own list of "long haul" essentials.

_____

_____

_____

_____

_____

_____

_____

_____

_____

PRINCIPLES FOR LIFE MANAGEMENT

Daily Essential Seven - WHO CARES?

Have you ever heard someone scream, 'I DON'T CARE," or maybe shout something like, "WHO CARES!" Are they really saying they don't care or are they implying they are not being heard. Could they seriously be suggesting that no one on the earth really cares, or are they frustrated at the moment by a lack of response? I know I have made both of these statements myself, but I did care and someone else cared as well. Both of these statements are self-centered at their core. We blurt them out in a fight to shut the other person out. We use them to leverage our emotions and feelings to get our own way. These declarations are made to evoke sympathy for us, or to shame the other persons ideas and perspectives. These are destructive words. These are prideful words. These are contentious words. They never bring unity. They rarely produce the results we had in mind.

Writing this makes me think of my grandsons. They will be getting along great until someone gets mad and blasts the other two with, "I DON'T CARE," while running out of the room. They can be competing in a game in which everyone is losing, throw up their hands and yell, "WHO CARES!" Children can be the masters of the "who cares" attitudes and proclamations, but married adults seem to be experts as well. A married couple can be on a date and the evening couldn't be better until one or the other gets their feelings hurt. Then here it comes, seemingly out of nowhere, "I DON'T CARE!" I wonder what would happen if we disciplined ourselves to respond, "You know I care a lot about our relationship. I'm so sorry I made you feel that way." What would the world of our relationship look like if we dropped these two phrases from our vocabulary? Co-workers might feel valued because they know someone cares. Friendships might grow stronger because there is a safe place for them. Volunteers might engage at a deeper level because their ideas are heard and their feedback is received. All because we are willing to restrain our self-centeredness, bridle our frustrations and replace " I don't care" with "I really care," and exchange "who cares" for "we care."

DAILY ESSENTIALS

HERE IS MY QUESTION: Do you care enough to care about not caring?

_____

_____

_____

_____

_____

_____

_____

_____

HERE IS MY CHALLENGE: Think about the times you have used either of these statements, write down the situation, now instruct yourself on a better response.

_____

_____

_____

_____

_____

_____

_____

_____

Daily Essential Eight - THROW IN THE TOWEL Part 1

My son and I both love boxing. I know it's a cruel sport but it's also Mano y Mano (man to man). One person's training vs another person's training. One boxer's corner against the other boxer's corner. One fighter's will vs the other's. The corner's job is to give strategy to the fighter throughout the fight, to medically attend to any cuts or swelling, to keep the fighter's psyche positively challenged, and to protect the fighter from unnecessary injury. When a fighter is in danger of serious injury, the corner will throw in their towel signaling to the referee that they are conceding the fight. Throwing in the towel is a last resort because it is a symbol of quitting. Quitting is not in the nature of a boxer. They are trained to press through pain, to overcome exhaustion, and to fight till the end. The fighter will always argue with their corner that they can go on with the battle.

I want to propose there are times when we need to throw in the towel. Battles where the enemy we face is greater than our capacity to defeat. Occasions when we throw in the towel to concede that our strength is spent and we have no more to give. You might ask, "Where is your faith"? My answer would be in the provision and wisdom of my corner team. I have a cut specialist that knows how to stop the bleeding. I have a good second who will refresh me between rounds. I have a great cornerman who will help me see what I don't see in the midst of the fight. However, unlike boxing, throwing in the towel does not stop the fight. We have an adversary who seeks to devour our lives, our purpose, and our relationship with God. Now we know that in the end that adversary is defeated. I'm not talking about throwing in the towel as a sign of defeat to the devil, but I am talking about throwing the towel in on myself. Recognizing that it's ok to admit that I cannot continue under the load of emotional stress, so I throw in the towel on my own mental powers and ask for the help of a counselor.

PRINCIPLES FOR LIFE MANAGEMENT

Understanding that at times I need to throw in the towel on my sin that easily besets me and get someone in my corner to patch me up to fight another day. I throw in the towel because I fight a war that is against principalities and powers, and I need the supernatural to touch my natural to overcome. I throw in the towel to acknowledge that greater is He that is in me, and through Him I can overcome the world. I throw in the towel because it's time to enter His rest, and let the Lord fight my battles. I am weak, but He is strong, so, I throw in the towel and become strong in the Lord and the power of His might!

1 Peter 5:6, (NLT) "So humble yourselves under the mighty power of God, and at the right time He will lift you up in honor" so, throw in the towel of pride.

DAILY ESSENTIALS

HERE IS MY QUESTION: Why are you holding onto a towel that requires you to fight in your own strength?

_____
_____
_____
_____
_____
_____
_____
_____

HERE IS MY CHALLENGE: Let go and throw in the towel!

_____
_____
_____
_____
_____
_____
_____
_____

Daily Essential Nine - THROW IN THE TOWEL - Part 2

No boxer wants his corner to throw in the towel signaling the referee that they are conceding the fight. They entered the ring to win. A boxer is a warrior not a quitter. The boxer's mindset is to battle to the end. Fighters believe they are champions not someone who gives up. However, their corner wants to protect their fighter from injury that could be career or life-threatening. The corner throws in the towel. The fight is over. Defeat is acknowledged. A loss is recorded. Why did they have to throw in the towel?

A fight begins long before the first bell rings. Every fighter goes to training camp for six to eight weeks. There they build their stamina through conditioning. They hone their skills through training, shadowboxing, and sparring. The camp also involves watching films of their opponent, strict dietary regiments, and getting free from outside distractions as much as possible. How the fighter prepares here has a lot to do with victory or defeat. Unlike boxing our fights are not scheduled. The Bible encourages us to be sober and aware because our adversary is like a roaring lions seeking its prey. Our opponent wants to catch us off guard so he can throw a sucker punch and take us out. We are challenged by scripture to be ready in season and out of season. How we prepare ourselves for spiritual battle has a lot to do with victory or defeat. Ultimately we win the war, but it is nice to win the battles along the way. The time to prepare is not when the bell rings or when the fight starts. Prep time has to be pre-fight. How we are preparing today will affect the outcomes of our fights tomorrow. We will never have to throw in the towel because Jesus destroyed the power of the devil through His death, burial, and resurrection. However, to enforce and sustain the victory He won for us, we have to train ourselves for battle. We accomplish this by building the stamina of our faith by being engaged in God's

Word. We get ready by honing our character through sharing the gospel and giving aid to the broken humanity around us. We develop our knockout punch by being aware of our opponent's strategies and strengthening ourselves through prayer and fasting. We sustain our focus by refusing to be caught up in worldly affairs or engaging in sin that is a setback. Our foe is defeated! Let's keep him that way by having a great training program!

DAILY ESSENTIALS

HERE IS MY QUESTION: What does your "training camp" regiment include?

_____

_____

_____

_____

_____

_____

_____

_____

_____

HERE IS MY CHALLENGE: Every great athlete has a trainer.... Find a trainer for your life... life coach, mentor, or counselor.

_____

_____

_____

_____

_____

_____

_____

_____

_____

DAILY ESSENTIALS

Daily Essential Ten - STABILITY IN MOTION

Have you ever had motion sickness? That nauseated feeling when you are riding through mountains on a curvy road in the back seat? Have you ever been on a cruise ship when an ocean storm hit? Your head spins, your stomach swirls, your face loses all its color and you have to spend the rest of the day in your cabin. Ok, how about that time when your dad or your uncle grabbed you by the ankles and spun you around and around and around and around. They stop but you don't. Everything is dizzy, you are disoriented, you are sick at your stomach, and you can't stand up. I'm sure all of us have experienced some type of motion sickness. Motion sickness pills can help but only if they are taken prior to the rise and fall of a roller coaster, or the turbulent waves of the sea, or the bumpy airplane flight. The pills can provide stability in motion.

Our lives are filled with motion as well. A day when we unexpectedly lose a job. Episodes of relational difficulties. Losses of loved ones or good friends. Seasons of financial stress. Life can be and will be filled with rough times. Jesus said, "I have told you all this so that you may have peace in me. Here on earth you will have many trials and sorrows. But take heart, because I have overcome the world." (John 16:33 NLT) We will have "life sickness" on occasion. The question is how do we find stability in the motions and nuances of life? Today, I want to propose two "life sickness pills" that may help. The first is the Word of God, the Bible. If consumed daily, prior to life events, the Word of God will stabilize your heart. It prepares you to see life from a biblical worldview, or to see life from God's perspective. The second is the power of prayer. Consider these verses, 1 John 5:14,15, "And this is the confidence that we have toward him, that if we ask anything according to his will he hears us. And if we know that he hears us in whatever we ask, we know that we have the requests that we have asked of him." Prayer petitions God's will in heaven to be realized here on earth.

Our daughter was born six weeks pre-mature and weighed only 3lbs 7oz. She spent five weeks in the ICU. We had no insurance and I was only making $600 per month. When the business office informed me that we were going to owe more than $20,000, I was hit with "life sickness". We had a daughter fighting for life. We had an overwhelming financial obligation we were not prepared to handle. However, fear was not able to crush me. We did have God's promises. We did have a relationship with God. The Word of God rose up and assured us that He meets all our financial needs. Our prayers and worship saw our daughter rebound and live through several critical moments. I am aware that not all life events turn out like ours. Bad things do happen to good people. However, even then, the Word of God and prayer will sustain us and see us through. The key is to build our lives on the Word and prayer daily, so that when life sickness does come, and it will, we are not overcome by it!

DAILY ESSENTIALS

HERE IS MY QUESTION: What life sickness hits you the hardest?

_____

_____

_____

_____

_____

_____

_____

_____

HERE IS MY CHALLENGE: Write down promises from the Word of God that speak to that life sickness, then pray those promises over your situations.

_____

_____

_____

_____

_____

_____

_____

_____

PRINCIPLES FOR LIFE MANAGEMENT

Daily Essential Eleven - FB LIVE, IG LIVE & RealTime YOU

Recently, I was in a local mall with my "Beautiful Rose of Texas" and took a seat in the food-court while she went into one of her favorite stores. Like a majority of those around me I jumped on my iPhone to scroll through all my social media apps. There were several teens to my right who were texting back and forth. Directly behind me was a couple of young boys playing video games. I looked up several times to see people almost collide because their eyes were on their phones.

It is amazing how many people live from digital post to digital post. Identities are shaped around the number of followers, likes, and views a person receives on social media. Email, texting, IM's, FB live, IG live, WhatsApp, and other digital applications have transitioned the landscape of relational interactions. The personal disconnect is evident when teens break up with each other on FB, employees quit their jobs through email, people leave their church and volunteer positions through texts. Many use these platforms to gossip, slander, criticize and demean others. Others feel empowered to pass judgement on everything from celebrities to the White House, from the pew to the pulpit, and from rumors to reality.

The digital world enables these forms of communications for good or bad. Zoom calls, webinars, and religious services online are common to our present world. The positive side is we are able to broaden the reach of our businesses, churches, interests, and information. The downside is we lose the intimacy that is involved in face-to-face interactions. The one-on-one moments where we share our space, our raw feelings, our significant accomplishments, and our personal struggles. The bible is filled with verses that encourage personal interaction; love one another, be kind to one another, forgive one another, and encourage one another. It also exhorts us not to forsake getting together, but to come together to share community and life.

So, my reflection today challenges me to reach out to the RealTime You and not your FB Live or your IG live. Your "RealTime" gives me the opportunity to touch you, to hear you, to see you, to know you, to believe in you, to care for you, to weep with you, to celebrate you, to honor you, and to journey with you through many seasons. That is relationship! That is personal!

DAILY ESSENTIALS

HERE IS MY QUESTION: Your Thoughts?

_____
_____
_____
_____
_____
_____
_____
_____
_____

HERE IS MY CHALLENGE: Take someone out for coffee and leave your phones in the car.

_____
_____
_____
_____
_____
_____
_____
_____
_____

Daily Essential Twelve - CLIMATE CHANGE

We have heard these words over and over, CLIMATE CHANGE, CLIMATE CHANGE! Whatever view you have on it, the truth is we could all benefit from taking a hard look at the climate of our own lives. What does it feel like to be around us? Does the atmospheric condition of our life damage those around us, or uplift them?

After taking a closer look at the condition of our lives, we may realize we need a CLIMATE CHANGE. What is the general trend of our attitudes, our perspectives, or our demeanor? Do we tend to see every glass half empty or half full? Can people be around us for any period of time and walk away better or do they see us later and want to avoid us? Are the prevailing winds of our life filled with bitterness or blessing? How do we view people, from a position of prejudice or from a posture of acceptance? When we show up, do we bring a raging storm or a gentle soaking rain? The ethos of who we are is seen before it is experienced.

Our "weather patterns" set the tone for our influence. The climate of our emotions generate the ability to care and empathize with others. The regularity of our devotions and intimacy with God empowers us to reach the unloveable. The atmospheric pressure of our will empowers us to choose to do good and not evil. The key to setting the climate change in our life is found in these verses: Psalms 139:23-24... make them a daily request and you will control the climate of your world.

DAILY ESSENTIALS

HERE IS MY QUESTION: Have you been living in the wrong climate?

_____

_____

_____

_____

_____

_____

_____

_____

_____

HERE IS MY CHALLENGE: Schedule a fast for 3, 7 or 21 days and seek God for His power to reset your life.

_____

_____

_____

_____

_____

_____

_____

_____

Daily Essential Thirteen - LISTEN BEFORE YOU SPEAK

Have you ever been in a conversation and wish you could take your words back? Sometimes the words that come out of our mouths even surprise us. We've heard the question, "Why do you have two ears and one mouth?" Answer: So you will listen twice as much as you speak. Listen Before You Speak is great advice for all of us. However, if you are like me you don't always heed the wisdom.

When I'm in conversations, I tend to be thinking of my response rather than listening to what is being said. My mind is recalling all the events of my life to come up with a "one-up" story of my own. Sometimes conversations get intense and I tend to want to defend myself. That's when I look into my wife's eyes and see the hurt she feels. That's when I become aware she wants me to care, to value her thoughts, to understand her pain, to hear her voice not just her words. That's when I wish I had Listened Before I Spoke! Conversations are a part of our daily life. Are we allowing the other person to be heard?

DAILY ESSENTIALS

HERE IS MY QUESTION: Who is crying out to be heard in your life?

_____

_____

_____

_____

_____

_____

_____

_____

HERE IS MY CHALLENGE: Take someone out to coffee and listen to them talk. When they pause, ask them a question that demands more than a yes or no answer. Repeat. Repeat. Repeat.

_____

_____

_____

_____

_____

_____

_____

_____

_____

Daily Essential Fourteen - DO WE REALLY KNOW?

I often make the statement, "There is someone waiting on you..." and I have found that to be true on so many levels. On the other side of your breakthrough, there are hurting people who are waiting on your freedom. Right now you may be halfway through a business plan, but people are already waiting on your product. There are people who have been waiting for my book, Essentials / Bridging the Leadership Gap, for years. The passion on the inside of you is for others as much as it is for you. That is why we have to keep moving today. We have to write another sentence. We have to meet with a coach or mentor. We have to invest our resources, time, energy and relational equity because they are waiting. **DO WE REALLY KNOW** who we are going to impact?

I remember the times I used to go out back to Mr. Felts' cow pasture. I would jump up on a stump and start preaching. His cows would be down by the creek in the shade chewing their cud. They would look up at me like, "There is that idiot again." I kept preaching. Soon one of them would get up and head my way. Then another would follow until soon the whole herd would be answering my altar call. **DID I REALLY KNOW** that years later I would be preaching to literally thousands and watching many of them answer the invitation?

What am I saying? It is simple. WE NEVER REALLY KNOW... but I promise someone is waiting on you right now. Maybe you have the gift of hospitality, and they are waiting on your smile. It could be that you repair cars, washing machines, or houses and they need you today! **You and I were created to make a difference.** Don't underestimate who you might impact tomorrow because of what is being developed in you today. **Pictured here** are some young pastors that I have the privilege to serve. Only one of them has known me more than ten years. It took the previous thirty-plus years for me to get ready to meet them.

I NEVER KNEW HOW I WOULD HELP THEM ONE DAY!

DAILY ESSENTIALS

HERE IS MY QUESTION: Why are you underestimating the possibilities of your life?

_____
_____
_____
_____
_____
_____
_____
_____
_____
_____

HERE IS MY CHALLENGE: Get on a stump and preach!

_____
_____
_____
_____
_____
_____
_____
_____
_____

PRINCIPLES FOR LIFE MANAGEMENT

Daily Essential Fifteen - HELP I NEED SOMEBODY!

I remember a season of my life where I was feeling very lonely. I had family who supported me and loved me but I felt isolated. There were friends who encouraged me and I knew they would help any way they could. It didn't help. I felt separated in the midst of all the love. I needed somebody, not just anybody (Beatles classic)! It was tough to admit. I had always been the pillar, the go to person, the problem solver. Now, I was unsure. This was in the midst of a season of incredible influence and responsibility. However, I was in a place that John Eldredge describes in his book *Wild at Heart*. I was wondering if I had what it took to be successful.

I think we all face seasons like this at times. We find ourselves in an inward struggle. The dream seems insurmountable for us. We measure our struggles, our weaknesses, and our lack against what we assume the mission will require. Yet, the reality is that God led us there and opened that door for us. He sees more in us than we see in ourselves. That is when we need somebody, not just anybody, but a confidant, an intimate soul, a trustworthy friend who God can use to call us out. We have to allow them into our deepest part of our humanity. The place where our soul is vulnerable and exposed. Why? Because we need freedom there so we can carry the vision with boldness. We need someone who knows the real, raw person we are and can speak light into our darkness. Let's stop kidding ourselves! We need somebody. Because when they show up, when they call us out, when they help us see where we are blind, then we will emerge free, confident, and courageous.

I have a friend who met me in that season, my best friend, Paul.

DAILY ESSENTIALS

HERE ARE MY QUESTIONS: Are you willing to invite someone into your secret place? Have you struggled long enough that you are ready for freedom? Until the pain of staying the same becomes greater than the pain of vulnerability, you will stay locked in your loneliness.

_____

_____

_____

_____

_____

_____

_____

_____

HERE IS MY CHALLENGE: Take the risk to allow somebody to become your trustworthy friend.

_____

_____

_____

_____

_____

_____

_____

_____

_____

PRINCIPLES FOR LIFE MANAGEMENT

Daily Essential Sixteen - WHY? WHY? WHY?

That is the question that always came to my mind whenever I was encouraged to write a book. I asked myself why because it was hard for me to believe anyone would want to read something I wrote. What would I write about anyway? But I kept being prodded by those close to me to write a book.

So, I had to answer the WHY?

I asked myself, "What am I passionate about?" Several things came to mind immediately: 1) I am passionate about the next generation 2) I am passionate about leadership 3) I am passionate about building leaders.

I asked myself, "What has been the center of my experiences?" It was easy to identify. Every organization I served put me in positions where I led generational teams. I led up to senior leaders and I develop young leaders. My strength as a strategist positioned me to build departments, create new initiatives, and pioneer new programs. Every team was comprised of young inexperienced leaders and seasoned leaders.

When I knew the why, I knew I had to write my first book, Essentials / Bridging the Leadership Gap.

WHY? Because I've watched young leaders crave mentorship. WHY? Because I've watched senior leaders overlook opportunities. *WHY? Because I've experienced the amazing dynamics when the leadership lid is lifted as both generations interact.*

DAILY ESSENTIALS

HERE ARE MY QUESTIONS: What is the WHY you need to answer before you unlock a dream, a new season, a new business, or a new you?

_____

_____

_____

_____

_____

_____

_____

_____

_____

HERE IS MY CHALLENGE: Write down your Why in ten words or less. Now get after it!

_____

_____

_____

_____

_____

_____

_____

_____

_____

PRINCIPLES FOR LIFE MANAGEMENT

Daily Essential Seventeen - IT'S THE PRINCIPLE OF THE THING

I used to live in a very small town in central Arkansas named Des Arc. The east side of Des Arc nestled up against the White River, so if you were to travel east you would have to cross a bridge to get to your destination. Many times heavy spring rains would cause the river to overflow. The banks would disappear, and you could see water standing in the fields and surrounding reservoirs. It always amazed me how the boundaries that were once there were erased. The river was lost under the floods. The river's identity was absorbed, and it no longer presented any sense of direction. The flood took away the life that once flourished along the riverbanks.

I wonder how many times the floods of life do the very same thing to us. We come into a season of heavy rainstorms. Our standards and convictions are challenged in the midst of the siege. Financial hardships, relational breakdowns, emotional stresses all pressing in to destroy us. If we are not careful, we haven't prepared ourselves. If we have neglected the warning signs, we may not even have a bridge to get us to the other side.

You've heard it said, **"It's the principle of the thing."** The thing is what presses against the principle. If there is no principle then the thing has no borders. No riverbanks if you will, and our lives begin to look like the flooded White River. The lesson herein: if we do not have sufficient principles that give perspective and guidance to us, then we will succumb to every storm of life. Principles pre-set our responses. Principles define us. Principles give us direction. Principles are the convictions we hold that will enable us to stand against temptations. You see, when the storms come, the height of our principles will determine the impact of the storms.

DAILY ESSENTIALS

HERE IS MY QUESTION: What are the defining principles that you live by and that create the standards of your life?

_____

_____

_____

_____

_____

_____

_____

_____

_____

HERE IS MY CHALLENGE: Review recent storms that you have endured and write down the principles that carried you through.

_____

_____

_____

_____

_____

_____

_____

_____

_____

PRINCIPLES FOR LIFE MANAGEMENT

Daily Essential Eighteen - OPTIONS | CHOICES | POSSIBILITIES

Several years ago I was put in a position to make a very difficult decision about my future. I was totally blindsided. Never saw it coming. I walked into my oversight's office and he informed me of the decision that had to be made. Ready or not... options, choices, and possibilities are on the table... choose wisely. I'm glad to report the outcome was beyond what I could have imagined.

There are times when life forces you to make a choice. You did not have that moment scheduled in your calendar. It showed up out of nowhere, like a thief in the night and now you are compelled to choose. You did not have any time to prepare yourself because you never saw this coming. An unannounced guest that is presenting you with choices you were unprepared to make. Depending on the seriousness of the decision, you may have to work through fear, insecurity, and uncertainty. You can feel like you've hit a dead-end and completely hopeless. You are alarmed because you are now being forced to move from what is familiar and comfortable to what is unknown and awkward. How we manage the options and possibilities in an unforeseen moment is critical for success. It is in these unforeseen moments where you are faced with the unimaginable. Where you have the opportunity to make decisions that can pivot you into a new season and a new direction.

These moments are scary at first, but they can become some of your greatest moments. It's in these times where we are forced to dig deep. We have to decide who we really are and who we want to become. These are the rubber hits the road type moments! Instances where we get to choose new possibilities, new opportunities and ultimately a new purpose. Several things to consider: 1) Let the Spirit of God govern your emotions, 2) Respond by faith not by fear, 3) Make the Word of God your reference point, 4) Get counsel from people who you trust, and 5) Honor the spiritual authority in your world.

DAILY ESSENTIALS

HERE IS MY QUESTION: What unforeseen circumstance has caught you off guard recently?

_____

_____

_____

_____

_____

_____

_____

_____

HERE IS MY CHALLENGE: Define what pivoted and changed on the other side of your choice and how it impacted your future.

_____

_____

_____

_____

_____

_____

_____

_____

Daily Essential Nineteen - WORTH / VALUE

How many times have you said to yourself, "This is not worth it?" You started with great expectations but then things became difficult. What you once thought was a great opportunity evolved into a worthless project. Maybe someone in your life made it deeply personal. They treated you like you weren't worth much. It could be that a coach, a parent, or another authority figure said that you wouldn't amount to much. You walked away feeling worthless. Much of what we assign to worth correlates to what we value most in life. For example, when the road becomes difficult, we want to quit because there is not enough perceived value for us to continue. Sometimes we carry the weight of being ostracized, so we demean our talents and the value they bring to our team. The challenge we have lies within two questions: Where do I find my worth? What are my values?

Many people attempt to find personal worth by securing a position/title, or by getting thousands of followers on their social media platforms, or by their physical appearance. Personal worth fluctuates by the circumstances that come their way. Scriptures tell us that we are fearfully and wonderfully created by God. Our worth is seen in the creative process because we are one of a kind. No one has your exact fingerprints, personality, or talents. You are special in the fact that you are unique. You carry that worth throughout eternity whether you walk in it or not.

It is also imperative that we understand our values. Values are the boundaries that keep us consistently on target to fulfill our purpose. When values are centered in selfishness, we tend to esteem things like wealth, position, winning, fame, authority, and success. None of those things are bad but selfishness drives them to dominance, greed, suppression, and pride. Our selfish purpose is to become the center of our universe. The opposite holds true when values are centered in serving others. Values that are established to promote generosity, serving, love, and compassion. The overwhelming purpose becomes living a life of self-sacrifice and open-handedness toward those around us. It's worth going the second mile because I value lifting the burdens of others. It's worth being generous because I value helping those in need. I serve willingly because I value the mission or the cause of my church, my company, or my city.

When we start asking ourselves, "Is this worth it?" It is probably a good time to ask ourself, "What value is motivating my decision?"

DAILY ESSENTIALS

HERE ARE MY QUESTIONS: What defines your personal worth? What are your values?

_____
_____
_____
_____
_____
_____
_____
_____
_____
_____

HERE IS MY CHALLENGE: Write down some opportunities that will let you live out your purpose and express your values.

_____
_____
_____
_____
_____
_____
_____
_____
_____

Daily Essential Twenty - TAKE THAT BACK

Remember that time you thought you had the best idea and it got shot down instantly by the whole team! Maybe you experienced a bully at school that tagged you with a nickname and it hurt you to the core. We grow up in a world that offends. Offenses are hurled at us without regard to the deep impact they have on our souls. We try to rise above the fray without losing our identity, but it is tough to handle. We want to shout like a little kid, **"TAKE THAT BACK!"** It is impossible to make light of being offended.

If being offended on one level or another is unavoidable, maybe **we should consider how we could benefit from an offense**. Let me suggest a couple of ideas for you. 1) Let the pain push you to self-reflect and see if there is an opportunity for personal growth. 2) Don't run from the criticism, run into it. Invite others to speak into the offense and uncover potential blind spots. 3) Refuse the pathway of unforgiveness because it will lock you into a never-ending attachment to the offense and offender. 4) Seek reconciliation where possible. **You never know what opportunities a reconciled relationship will open for you in the future. Don't burn your bridges.**

DAILY ESSENTIALS

HERE IS MY QUESTION: What baggage are you carrying from an unresolved offense?

_____

_____

_____

_____

_____

_____

_____

_____

HERE IS MY CHALLENGE: Make a list of unresolved offenses and then determine how you should respond to each one.

_____

_____

_____

_____

_____

_____

_____

_____

_____

PRINCIPLES FOR LIFE MANAGEMENT

Daily Essential Twenty-one - WHO'S GOT THE TOWEL?

My grandsons love to play "king of the mountain" with me. It started with the number one grandson, Judah, who loved to jump on me with his famous, "banana bunch thing a ma jig." The objective is to be the last one on the bed and claim the title, "king of the mountain! (KOM)" I recently retired from the game being 64 years old with three grandsons, twelve, eight, and five. It was simply a matter of life or death.

We have a tendency to strive to be "king of our mountains" in one way or another. There seems to be a sense of self-validation when we achieve KOM status. We want to win every time, which in and of itself is unrealistic. The pursuit of KOM status can lead us to take advantage of others. It can motivate us to use our authority or power unscrupulously. We can even compete by stacking the deck in our favor. There is a means to hold ourselves in check. The best example of this is found in what we know as the "Last Supper." Jesus is with His disciples for the last meal and something unique happens. He takes a bowl of water and a towel and begins to wash the disciples' feet. If you remember, Jesus told them earlier that the greatest (KOM) in the kingdom of God would be the servant of all. Now He models for them exactly what that looks like with towel in hand.

When we reach for a towel before a crown, we position ourselves to think of others instead of ourselves. The crown is to exalt us. **The towel is about helping others.** The crown is about others serving us. The towel is about us serving them. Serving doesn't appeal to those who see success as being on the top, but serving positions you to have greater influence by assisting others to accomplish their dreams.

DAILY ESSENTIALS

HERE IS MY QUESTION: Do You Have a Towel?

_____
_____
_____
_____
_____
_____
_____
_____
_____

HERE IS MY CHALLENGE: Crown or Towel?

_____
_____
_____
_____
_____
_____
_____
_____

PRINCIPLES FOR LIFE MANAGEMENT

Daily Essential Twenty-two - HOPE TO COPE

Have you ever heard yourself say, "I Hope So?" You may have said it in the context of needing a personal breakthrough. Maybe you were questioning if a person could be trusted. Behind the expression there is usually something or someone whom we have concerns with or reservations about. "I Hope So," is our search for faith and confidence that enables us to cope with the stress in play. The scriptures warn us that hope deferred makes the heart sick. We need to have a sense that there is light at the end of the tunnel in which we find ourselves. It would be nice if there was a "hope pill" we could take for hopeless conditions. The daily reality that we encounter is that hope is needed for us to advance and succeed.

So, what are some things that can awaken hope in our situations. What immediately comes to mind is the story of David and Goliath. David went out as a young shepherd boy to face a giant who was an experienced warrior. Before entering the battle, David recalled that he had killed a lion and a bear. There are moments in our history where we either experienced victory or knew of someone in a similar situation who came out on top. Recalling these successful outcomes can give us the optimism we need to move forward.

Another source of hope comes from David's story as well. You remember that Saul tried to put his suit of armor on David to make him a warrior. Well, it didn't fit. David took his sling, gathered five smooth stones from the brook, and slew the giant with his own set of skills. He trusted what he knew. He trusted his weapon. His sling was good enough to kill the lion and the bear. Now, it was good enough to kill a giant. Hope can be renewed when we realize that what we have is enough to get us through.

The final thing we can learn from David was his faith in God.

He declared to the giant that he was coming to him in the name of the God of Israel. His hope was in the God whom he worshipped while tending his sheep. The God whose promises are in Him yes and in Him amen. Hope is restored when we understand that the battle is not ours but His. Hope anchors itself in our souls when we remember His Word and apply it to our situation. Hope to cope lives in us. We simply have to recall our victories, trust in what we have, and remember His faithfulness.

DAILY ESSENTIALS

HERE IS MY QUESTION: What is challenging your hope?

_____
_____
_____
_____
_____
_____
_____
_____
_____

HERE IS MY CHALLENGE: Write down your victories, list your talents, and remember some of His promises that apply.

_____
_____
_____
_____
_____
_____
_____
_____
_____

DAILY ESSENTIALS

Daily Essential Twenty-three - WHERE IS THE REMOTE

Have you ever come home wanting to chill after a hard day? On the ride home, you're thinking about the TV series you recorded. You're excited to catch up on all the action. When you arrive at the house you take a hot shower straight away, get into your favorite pj's, and prepare for the downtime ahead. You ate on the way home, so you decide to pop some popcorn for your "night at the movies." Now you are all set! Where's the remote? You look through the couch cushions. You search under all the furniture. You hunt for it in all the cabinets and drawers. No remote. You yell out, "Whose got the remote?" "Does anyone in this house know where the remote is?" Silence.

Has life ever felt like that to you? You're all pumped and excited for something you've been dreaming about for days. You feel like you've done everything in your power to prepare yourself. You've even gone the extra mile on several occasions. The time arrives. However, you are informed that you are missing one thing (sounds like a trip to the DMV!). You feel like you've been working on a 1,000-piece puzzle and one piece has gone missing. It is nowhere to be found. You are frustrated, angry, disappointed, and absolutely sick inside.

The Bible speaks to moments like these in Proverbs 13:12, "Hope deferred makes the heart sick, But when the desire comes, it is a tree of life." When the very thing we greatly anticipated doesn't happen, it's a let down. We have all had these moments, moments where we can't find the remote or the puzzle piece is lost, and life sucks. However, most of us stop quoting the verse with the line "hope deferred makes the heart sick." Yet, the verse goes on to say, "when the desire comes" and that makes all the difference. When we do find the remote after a vigorous search, when we do discover where the last piece of the puzzle is, then the joy factor is multiplied a million times over than just walking in and turning on the show or finishing the puzzle.

Sometimes the deferred things in life can feel so final. Sometimes being put on hold seems unfair. When we experience delay we can project a negative outcome. What if the deferral is really a preparation season? A pause that is setting some things in order so that the when the desire comes it has more to offer? I'll close with this. Recently, I ordered some author copies of my new book to sell. They were to arrive a couple of weeks or so before an event I had scheduled to sell them. They did not show. Day after day I was looking for delivery. No books! I checked the tracking number, they are late but they are coming! Then I get a notice from the company. If the books don't arrive by tomorrow, we will refund you. If they arrive after we refund you, you can keep them, destroy them, or return them. That is exactly what happened. I was refunded my cost on the books, but able to keep them because they arrived the day before the event (a week after the refund). So, if you can't find the remote, keep looking, YOU MAY BE IN FOR A BIG SURPRISE!

DAILY ESSENTIALS

HERE IS MY QUESTION: How do you handle the delayed things in your life?

_____

_____

_____

_____

_____

_____

_____

_____

HERE IS MY CHALLENGE: Next time delay comes your way, breathe and put your trust in the God who brings the desire at the right moment.

_____

_____

_____

_____

_____

_____

_____

_____

PRINCIPLES FOR LIFE MANAGEMENT

Daily Essential Twenty-four - ALWAYS FRESH

I recently ate at a seafood restaurant that promised from catch to your table in twenty-four hours. I have to admit the salmon was the best I had ever tasted. There was a vast difference between it and any I had eaten at a normal seafood chain. Even the filet was cut differently which made its presentation superb. Many grocery chains have similar offers, fresh from the farm to your table. It gives you the sense that you are buying directly from farmer Jones. You are sold on totally organic.

When I think about this concept it makes me wonder how fresh is my life? When I show up to be a husband, am I stale? If a friend comes to me for advice, do I bring an original perspective? Do I take comfort and solace in being routine or do I keep myself aggressive and current? I also thought about what is required to keep it "always fresh." You have to contend with supply and delivery. Where do I get my supply to support life's demands? What is the delivery mechanism so that I can offer my best?

All of this brought me back to two fundamentals. Number one is understanding that fresh comes from the original. The salmon came from the river and the groceries came from the farm. My freshness comes from daily communion with my Father in heaven. He is my creator. Secondly, delivery requires transportation. It has to get from the origin to the end user either by trucking, shipping, rail, or other means. In my case, it comes through the Word and the Spirit. I am able to be my best as a husband, a friend, a consultant, a parent, and a grandparent when the Word of God and the Spirit of God directs my actions and decisions. At the end of the day, "always fresh" is about customer satisfaction. It is giving the customer an experience they cannot find in the generic product line. There are customers interacting with us every day. It might be a co-worker, a spouse, a family member, or the person in the seat next to us on a plane. So, I have to continually ask myself, "How fresh is my life?"

DAILY ESSENTIALS

HERE IS MY QUESTION: What is your customer base experiencing? Fresh or Stale?

_____
_____
_____
_____
_____
_____
_____
_____

HERE IS MY CHALLENGE: Rate your freshness over the next ten days on a scale of one (molded) to ten (always fresh).

_____
_____
_____
_____
_____
_____
_____
_____

Daily Essential Twenty-five - THE DANGER OF CONFORMITY

I remember as kids we used to play with Play-Doh. It was a putty type product that you squeezed into plastic molds. We would remove the dough and bake it in the oven. Once it was baked it lost its pliability and remain fixed in the molded state. You could no longer shape it or press it into a different mold.

Sometimes our lives are like that. We begin a stage of life with great flexibility and promise. We can choose our way through without being influenced into any permanent position. Then, someone enters our life with a "plastic mold" that they feel we need to be pressed into. They press us with words intending to leverage their perspective and conform us into their prototype. We need to remember it's their template not ours. Culture also has a way of trying to conform us. The world around us challenging our values or convictions. The loudest voices in the crowd trying to shape the narrative of who we are to be. Hurts and wounds also try their best to shape us into a pseudo image of ourselves. They tell us we are failures. Brokenness describes us as rejects. Relational betrayals endeavoring to seal us into an image of unloveable.

The danger of conformity is that it becomes like a baked mold of clay. It locks us into a fixed state of a lie. We must recall that we are fearfully and wonderfully crafted by the Creator of heaven and earth. We have been fashioned in His image for good works. He does not make mistakes. We must be transformed by renewing our mind to the truth of His Word. It is in the alignment with truth, His truth, that we find freedom from conformity. Why narrow your purpose to the perspective of another person? You have so much more in you than they can see. Why let culture press you to follow the crowd? You are unique and your voice is legitimate. Why allow the hardships of life to shape you with their lies? You are beautiful and deserve the freedom of truth. Enter the journey of transformation and discover life on the other side of conformity.

DAILY ESSENTIALS

HERE IS MY QUESTION: Where have you conformed to a "plastic mold" and what lie have you believed as a result?

_____

_____

_____

_____

_____

_____

_____

_____

HERE IS MY CHALLENGE: Break the mold!

_____

_____

_____

_____

_____

_____

_____

_____

PRINCIPLES FOR LIFE MANAGEMENT

Daily Essential Twenty-six - ALIGNMENT MATTERS

Have you ever driven a car out of alignment? It can be a scary experience. I owned a 1966 baby blue Ford Galaxy my freshman year of college. It was eight years old at the time. One day a classmate asked me to take him to a job interview. He did not know that my frontend was completely out of alignment. If I had to slam on the brakes, the car would veer hard right without any warning. Sure enough we were heading back on a downhill street and the light suddenly changed. I had to hit on the brakes to avoid the car in front. We slammed hard into the curb on his side of the car. Upon impact, he looked at me, I smiled, the light changed and I continued driving back to campus.

When a car is out of alignment we take it to the shop, but what happens when our life is out of sync? Where do we turn? How do we position ourselves for re-alignment? Have you ever had reservations about taking your car to the shop? You worry if they will be honest. You have concerns about their expertise. We can have those same apprehensions about getting help for ourselves. The alignment of our car matters, but the alignment of our life matters more.

Here are a few considerations. First, we need to make sure our relationship with God is healthy. He is the "Great Mechanic" if you will. He knows everything about us, and He is always available to help in time of need. Secondly, we need to realize God uses people. So, we need to ask ourselves if we have the right relational alignments. Someone made this observation about relationships; if Satan wants to destroy a person he sends them an evil relationship, if God wants to restore and build a person He sends them a wise relationship. Healthy relationships are vital to restoration. Thirdly, we must seek out those skilled and trained to help be it a counselor, a pastor, a mentor, a coach, or a consultant. Find someone who you can trust because you cannot continue to live with a crushed spirit. Lastly, we must understand that we can't ignore it, and it will go away. We have to admit that we have a problem. We need alignment. Otherwise, we will never lean into God, evaluate our relationships or seek out professional assistance.

My 1966 baby blue Ford Galaxy needed alignment, and I was putting lives in jeopardy. I wonder how many lives we put at risk because we won't take ourselves into the shop for repairs?

DAILY ESSENTIALS

HERE IS MY QUESTION: What did this writing speak to you?

_____
_____
_____
_____
_____
_____
_____
_____
_____

HERE IS MY CHALLENGE: Alignment Matters.

_____
_____
_____
_____
_____
_____
_____
_____
_____

Daily Essential Twenty-seven - YOU ARE VALUABLE

Can you hear a statement like that and believe it? Read it again:
You are Valuable! Many of us have a hard time with a
statement so forthright and declarative. We tend to filter it
through experiences of our past where we felt rejected. Times
where someone said we would never amount to anything.
Moments when we tried and failed at something. Seasons
where we were overlooked for a promotion or an award. I
recall a night when I was about twelve years old. They were
announcing the all stars for our local little league. I was sure
my name would be called. I had the highest batting average in
the league. A twelve-year-old does not understand small town
politics. I didn't realize my failure to make it to a lot of team
practices would influence my coach's decision to withdraw my
name. My name was never called. I jumped on my Schwinn
bicycle and peddled as fast as I could crying all the way home.

You may have had a similar experience. A point in time where
someone's actions or words defined you. We have all had
negative encounters and been the recipients of flippant words.
Some of us have carried those "defining moments" all our
lives. Those lies that imprisoned us to live beneath our true
self. Those deceptions that destroyed our self-worth. The good
news is that you and I are valuable. We can break out from
under the fraudulent pretenses and live in truth. We begin by
believing what God says about us. Psalm 139:14 declares that
we are fearfully and wonderfully made. The Message Bible puts
it this way, "Body and soul, I am marvelously made." We are
His craftsmanship, and He does not make any junk. He created
us for a specific purpose in this generation.

Why should we allow a created person determine our created
purpose? Why should we allow a human experience define our
spiritual destiny? We may have failed, but we are not failures.
Whoever said we would never amount to anything did not

know God said different. You are Valuable! Hear that today!
You are Valuable! Believe that today! You are Valuable! Live
like it today!

DAILY ESSENTIALS

HERE IS MY QUESTION: What has consistently disputed your value?

_____

_____

_____

_____

_____

_____

_____

_____

HERE IS MY CHALLENGE: Write down the words or experiences that demeaned your value. Now list the lie that was spoken or experienced. Finally, list the truth about yourself.

_____

_____

_____

_____

_____

_____

_____

_____

_____

PRINCIPLES FOR LIFE MANAGEMENT

Daily Essential Twenty-eight - I LOVE US

Have you ever been around someone who always takes a second or third look at themselves in the mirror? I mean the person who wasn't looking for a hair out of place, but the person who lingered to admire themselves. Some of us have a family member who always has to be first in everything; storytelling, buffet line, games. Maybe we know a co-worker who champions themselves because they really believe they are the best at everything. Bottom line is that these people are in love with themselves. When we step back and think about our relationship with them we don't enjoy being around them. People in love with themselves are usually arrogant, rude, self-centered, and stingy. They rarely see the needs around them. They demand more than they contribute. These self-lovers are blind to the hurt and pain they tend to inflict upon others. Maybe at their core they are not a bad person but the good that might be there is lost in their demeanor and actions. If we are honest, all of us have areas of "I love me!"

I recently saw a throw pillow with this inscription, "I love us." My first thought was about my relationship with the Beautiful Rose of Texas. We've been married forty-four years and both of us would say, "I love us!" We have traversed through many seasons both good and bad. Each of us would say, "I Love Us" because we have made each other better through the years. Then I thought about the privilege I have had to serve on some amazing teams. Teams that really valued and cared for each other. Teams that respected each other's contribution and cheered each other on in the process. Teams that would say at the end of the day, "I Love Us!" Lastly, I thought about those who have no "Us." Their lives torn by circumstances beyond their control. I thought about the disenfranchised who never had a dad or mom. I remembered those addicted and enslaved by drugs and alcohol. My heart broke for the outcasts in society who look different, talk different, and live different. Who will come to their aid? Who will take on the challenge to come alongside and be an "us" for them? What would our world be like if we could change the "I Love Me" to "I Love Us?"

DAILY ESSENTIALS

HERE IS MY QUESTION: Who has been the "Us" for you? How did their role in your life make a difference?

_____

_____

_____

_____

_____

_____

_____

_____

_____

HERE IS MY CHALLENGE: Find someone who needs you today… help them experience a moment of "I Love Us."

_____

_____

_____

_____

_____

_____

_____

_____

_____

Daily Essential Twenty-nine - EACH STEP CLOSER

Recently I was having lunch with a coworker. We finished lunch and were returning to our cars when I noticed he was about fifteen feet in front of me. How did he get so far ahead so fast? I realized that for every stride he took I was having to take at least two. Each step we took brought us closer to our vehicles, but our arrival time would certainly be different. Had he not slowed down, he would have beaten me by half a block easily.

Take this same thought and apply it to our lives. Every day we are moving toward something. Each step moves us closer to our objective. Every time we advance the dream draws nearer. We may not have the same pace as those around us, but we are progressing all the same. We have to forge ahead to make headway. Sometimes our journey requires steps of faith. We have to reach past any pain and press on. The path ahead may have stop signs, crosswalks, and oncoming traffic, but we cannot sit down if we want to reach our destination. Each action brings more clarity, each stride moves us beyond barriers, and every step forward contributes to a successful outcome.

Those who choose to push ahead make their dreams possible. Fulfilling our purpose requires putting one foot in front of the other. Enterprises call for daily movement. We cannot arrive without gaining ground. If we want to write a book, we have to write a sentence. If we want to climb a mountain, we have to gather our climbing gear. If we want to start a business, we have to draft a proposal. Life's ambitions can only be accomplished by the actions of those who aspire to accomplish them. We cannot be discouraged with incremental steps. We cannot sellout to complacency or apathy. We must take the next step. We have to move.

DAILY ESSENTIALS

HERE IS MY QUESTION: Are you in stride with your dreams?

_____

_____

_____

_____

_____

_____

_____

_____

HERE IS MY CHALLENGE: Compile a list of action items needed for your next step.

_____

_____

_____

_____

_____

_____

_____

_____

Daily Essential Thirty - PAYDIRT

Hitting "pay dirt" is an idiom from the mid-1800s and refers to a miner finding gold or other precious metals while sifting soil. You may recall an old western movie where a miner comes screaming into town, "I hit paydirt!" When we think about the concept of paydirt, we think of something that has to be discovered. Paydirt contains valuable resources within it, but those resources have to be sifted from the dirt before they are exposed.

There is a process to uncover what is beneath the surface. Certain tools are used to simplify the procedure and make the work much easier. Different soils contain different reserves of wealth and therefore require different strategies for mining. Once paydirt is discovered, it produces riches that make the tedious and hard work worthwhile.

Most of us are searching for paydirt. Our paydirt may be a job opportunity. Some of us may be looking to discover our God-given purpose. We could be in pursuit of a close friendship, a marriage partner, or a business connection. The treasure we seek is largely determined by a season of life we find ourselves. Paydirt for a young married couple might be having a child. Senior adults might be looking for security, or legacy, or better health. Entrepreneurs need investors. Politicians need votes. Our pursuits for paydirt can be filled with excitement followed by disappointment, obstacles that lead to a breakthrough, big paydays or bankruptcy, or huge highs and crashing lows. We are willing to take the journey because paydirt may involve high risks but it also offers a high reward.

Paydirt fills life with excitement. Paydirt offers a mysterious journey into the unknown. Paydirt keeps us guessing, hoping, sifting, investing, working, and searching. Paydirt is our purpose, our vision, our goal, our passion. So, as the old miners would say, "Thar's gold in them thar hills!"

DAILY ESSENTIALS

HERE IS MY QUESTION: What is Your Paydirt?

_____
_____
_____
_____
_____
_____
_____
_____
_____

HERE IS MY CHALLENGE: Run after it and one day you will hear yourself saying, "I hit PAYDIRT!"

_____
_____
_____
_____
_____
_____
_____
_____
_____

Daily Essentials

Part Two
Chasing Dreams

DAILY ESSENTIALS

Daily Essential One - SPEAKING BETWEEN THE LINES

There is a strong biblical admonition for a person to let their "yes be yes" and their "no be no." Another truth from the Bible states that people should speak the truth in love. Each of these directives are given so that relationships can have clarity and accountability. However, most of us are experts of what I call "speaking between the lines." We hide the truth in our conversations for fear of offending, or for the sake of hiding our true feelings. We couch our yes or no in between statements that leave us a way out. Honor and respect are lost in sarcasm and criticism. Commitment is hedged by excuses.

This is not always done with ill intent but sometimes just out of fear and past experiences. Speaking between the lines can also be silence. A word is never spoken, but everyone in the room knows what the person is saying. They roll their eyes, shake their heads, or sit with a disposition of indifference. It is as if they are shouting disapproval, but with a smile on their face. Their yes becomes a no when they leave the room. Dishonesty wins the day either because of their pride or their fear. Speaking between the lines never allows unity to be achieved.

James, the brother of Jesus, takes it a step further when he writes, "For we all stumble and sin in many ways. If anyone does not stumble in what he says [never saying the wrong thing], he is a perfect man [fully developed in character, without serious flaws], able to bridle his whole body and rein in his entire nature [taming his human faults and weaknesses]. Jesus himself said, "Out of the abundance of the heart the mouth speaks." Speaking between the lines is a heart issue. Because our hearts have been wounded in the past, we speak between the lines of that hurt. When our hearts have experienced rejection, we speak between the lines of that rejection. The heart, therefore, is the key to breaking the curse of speaking between the lines. It is from a place of freedom and healing that we are able to speak the truth in love. A secure heart allows us to commit to making our yes, yes and our no, no.

DAILY ESSENTIALS

HERE IS MY QUESTION: How is your heart today?

_____

_____

_____

_____

_____

_____

_____

_____

_____

HERE IS MY CHALLENGE: Find a place of solace and ask Father to heal your heart. Follow-up by sharing your struggle with someone you can trust for counsel and prayer.

_____

_____

_____

_____

_____

_____

_____

_____

PRINCIPLES FOR LIFE MANAGEMENT

Daily Essential Two - DREAM, DREAM, DREAM

Have you ever been in a class or a seminar and the presenter asks you this question, "If money was no obstacle and you knew you could not fail, what would you do?" It's easy to imagine yourself doing something incredible when you envision what could be through that perspective. You take all the lids off and you dream without fear. Why, because resources are not an issue and you cannot do anything else but succeed! When assumed restrictions are removed, there are no limitations to the possibilities.

What if you were told right now to "dream without fear"? Would you respond with the same type of faith, or would you immediately realize there are obstacles in the way? Would you think about your bank account and the deficit of having enough to resource your ideas? Would you put the lids back on, lock up your dreams, and put them back on the shelf? What reasons would you give to shut down starting a business, writing a book, getting married, planting a church, helping the poor, furthering your education, running for offices, leading a company, or venturing out of your comfort zone?

DAILY ESSENTIALS

HERE IS MY QUESTION: Why are you afraid to dream without fear?

_____

_____

_____

_____

_____

_____

_____

_____

_____

HERE IS MY CHALLENGE: Write down your dream. Now write down one thing you could do each day for the next seven days to move toward fulfilling your dream. Repeat each week for the next year.

_____

_____

_____

_____

_____

_____

_____

_____

_____

Daily Essential Three - FIGHT FOR YOUR FUTURE NOT YOUR PAST!

What is behind us has already been lived. It is our history but it is not our destiny. Our ambitions should never center around recreating what was and we should never aspire to return to "the good ole days." **When we focus on the past we waste the opportunities we have today.** It is like driving down the highway looking constantly in our rear view mirror! It will not get us to the destination we desire. A great example of this is the story of Israel coming out of 400 years of bondage in Egypt. They come to a difficult place on their journey to the promised land. Instead of keeping their eyes on their future they turn their hearts and minds back to what was behind. You know you are in a bad place when you think the slavery of your past has now become your happy place!

Fight for your future. Sure we will face difficulties. There will be people who challenge us. Circumstances will not always be in our favor. Resources may be scarce. But there is still a future and a hope that God has for us. Fight for your future! Press through the doubt and unbelief. Push back the fear and frustration! You have some great days ahead of you!

Learn from your past but don't live there. Let the past be a reference for you, but don't let it be your purpose. Fight for your future! Your past is visited by memory, but your future is visited by expectation. David remembered when he killed a lion and a bear, but now he faced a giant. Listen to his expectation, "I will strike you and take your head from you!" He fought for his future! Fight for yours!

My journey to write my first book, Essentials / Bridging the Leadership Gap, was filled with obstacles. I had to fight fear. I had to confront distractions. I had to combat insecurity. I had to battle through my lack of knowledge. I had to navigate unfamiliar technologies.

I had to fight for my future.

DAILY ESSENTIALS

HERE IS MY QUESTION: Will your dream, your mission, your passion be cemented in your past or will you fight for your future?

_____

_____

_____

_____

_____

_____

_____

_____

_____

_____

HERE IS MY CHALLENGE: Dream big enough to know you can't get there without a fight!

_____

_____

_____

_____

_____

_____

_____

_____

_____

Daily Essential Four - CAMPFIRE STORIES

There is nothing like sitting in pitch dark with close friends around a good campfire. The fire supplies just enough light to see your companions. The fire provides the right mood and a relaxed setting. Then comes the storytelling! Whoever says, "only your hairdresser knows" has never sat around a campfire and heard some of the tall tales told there. Each adventure challenged by the next person's one-up narrative. The pop and crackle of the hot fire sends sparks up through the opening of the tall trees surrounding the camp. Certain types of wood burn hotter and provide more sparks than others. If you have a nice still night, that is a little overcast, the embers glow brightly as they emerge from the smoke and flames of the fire. It's interesting to see how high they get before they burn out.

The conversations of life can be like those at a campsite. Talk around the office, hallway discussions, phone calls between friends, social media posts, family exchanges around the dinner table or meetings at the local coffee shop, all have the propensity to start a good fire. When you add in the right topic, or you embellish the facts a little, or you leave out a portion of the truth, you can intensify the heat and create more sparks. Sparks that take awhile to burn out. Embers that can become destructive if they fall into dry and parched foliage. Fires that inflame shame, rejection, judgement, criticism, anger, and negativity would rage and leave a charred desolation behind. That's the negative side. However, if we put ourselves in the same context, but changed the topics, spoke honorably, valued honesty, and made it a point to listen before we speak, the outcome would be vastly different. Sparks of truth would light up a world unlike any other. Fires that spark affirmation, inclusion, esteem, respect, love, and optimism would illuminate the greatness, the potential, and the value in others.

The old campfire song rings true, "it only takes a spark, to get a fire going," and that spark is deadly or life-giving. It all depends on what kind of campfire story we want to tell.

DAILY ESSENTIALS

HERE IS MY QUESTION: Have you ever been affected by a campfire story? How did it make you feel (one negative feeling, one positive feeling)?

_____

_____

_____

_____

_____

_____

_____

_____

HERE IS MY CHALLENGE: Find someone who has been negatively impacted by a campfire story and start a positive fire in their life.

_____

_____

_____

_____

_____

_____

_____

_____

_____

PRINCIPLES FOR LIFE MANAGEMENT

Daily Essential Five - LIVE WITHOUT LIMITS

My son is an adventurer. However, there have been several times that fear held him back. It became the thing that limited his experiences and possibilities. I can still remember the day he called us and said he was determined to overcome his fears. Ok. "I'm going skydiving!" I guess that's one way to overcome the fear of heights. Another time he was determined to overcome his fear of sharks. No, he didn't get into a shark tank, but he did take a wave runner seven miles off the shore into the middle of the Pacific. Then he jumped off and swam around. I guess he overcame sharks, whales, dolphins, and all other sea creatures. He determined that life was not going to hold him back any longer.

The point is we all have things in our life that seek to limit us. Those hurdles and barriers that want to keep us shut inside. Constraints can enter our lives through cruel conversations that wound us. The words penetrate our souls and set up negative images of ourselves. Many times a bad experience can define us as a failure. We approach new opportunities with reservations because we fear that we will replay that incident. If we are not mindful of these things, we find ourselves capped by our past, by what others say, or by images of failure. We can live our lives fenced in and barricaded off from anything that even remotely scares us, living within our comfort zone or we can determine to **live without limits**.

What if we did just that, determined to **live without limits**? What if we decided to raise the roof? What if we truly took to heart Philippians 4:13, "I can do everything through Christ who gives me strength"? What if we faced our setbacks? What if we determined today that we are going to live without limits? I wonder what accomplishments would be realized? What if we embraced the stretch, leaned into the uncomfortable, and welcomed the newness to come.

95

DAILY ESSENTIALS

HERE IS MY QUESTION: What if?

_____
_____
_____
_____
_____
_____
_____
_____
_____
_____

HERE IS MY CHALLENGE: Make two columns on a page. In the first column, list your challenges. In the second column, define what life would look like when that challenge was overcome.

_____
_____
_____
_____
_____
_____
_____
_____
_____

PRINCIPLES FOR LIFE MANAGEMENT

Daily Essential Six - RIGHT LANE MUST EXIT

Do you love to travel? Seeing the sights and sounds of places you've never been to before? My wife and I live in Michigan and we love to take drives. Recently, we went to the beautiful Traverse City and found a place that makes the best pies in the world. Ok. We knew it was there and made the two hours plus drive just for their pies. There have been other times when we've been driving through a city unfamiliar to us. Maybe you've found yourself in the same predicament. You are on a multi-lane road and happen to be in the right lane. Traffic is bumper to bumper and you are confronted with a sign that reads: "Right lane must Exit." You have no choice but to take the exit. Now you have to get Siri on the phone to map out a route to your original destination. The kids are crying, everyone is hungry, and you are lost. Which problem to solve first? Eating of course which will alleviate two of the three issues. All the chain restaurants are fast food so, you decide to take a chance on a locally-owned cafe. Jackpot! You've just discovered the families' newest favorite place to eat and it's within a reasonable driving distance from home.

I wonder how many times life has given us a "Right Lane Must Exit" detour? How do we handle those interruptions to our plans? Do we fear the moment because we know we are lost? Are we stubborn and refuse to involve Siri? Are we determined to find our own way back? Then the realization comes that our actions are affecting others who are with us. They have needs and they are frustrated. Right lane exits are not always easy off, easy on experiences. Sometimes they take us to a place we would have never ventured. They can actually cause us to discover something that becomes a part of our future. The exit seemed to be a mishap, but on the other side of it was new adventure, a new destination, and a new desire. Maybe the next time we encounter the same circumstances we can take a breath and enjoy the journey.

Could it be that the exit wasn't necessarily in our plans, however it was exactly what God planned for us? What if we invited the Holy Spirit to lead us through the maze? Do you think this could possibly be true: Right Lane Must Exit = The Steps of the Righteous are Ordered by the Lord? We don't stop traveling just because we had a detour. God has a Future and a Hope for us!

DAILY ESSENTIALS

HERE IS MY QUESTION: What exits do you remember that God used to advance you to the next level of life?

_____

_____

_____

_____

_____

_____

_____

_____

_____

HERE IS MY CHALLENGE: Write down the exits that God had you take and list the things you learned or the people you met. Now tell someone your story.

_____

_____

_____

_____

_____

_____

_____

_____

DAILY ESSENTIALS

Daily Essential Seven - IT'S NONE OF YOUR BUSINESS

Several years ago a couple of friends got at odds with each other. The impasse started over a mistake made by one of the friends while under some intense stress. When the other friend came in to give aid, their intentions and motives came under scrutiny. It was a sad situation to watch the two grow farther and farther apart. What had been a close friendship for several years now seemed hopeless to restore.

The schism was intensified as other well-meaning confidants took sides in the breach. Rumors, assumptions, accusations, half-truths, and outright lies began to consume the two communities and erode the possibility of restoration between the two former best friends. The chasm grew daily as criticisms were fueled by gossip, slander, and threats of retaliation. The more people got involved the wider the separation between the two increased.

Fortunately, some seasoned leaders respected by both friends were able to intervene and help reconcile the relationship. However, many of those who took sides were wounded in the conflict and never recovered. Some are living in bitterness even to this day. They got involved in something that was none of their business, and it took them out. I've watched this scenario play out numerous times where the two initial players repair the breach, but the peripheral players never have the opportunity.

Proverbs 26:17 says, "Interfering in someone else's argument is as foolish as yanking a dog's ears." The Message Bible puts it this way, "You grab a mad dog by the ears when you butt into a quarrel that's none of your business." I am not saying we don't empathize with our friends and comfort them in their brokenness. However, to take up their offense is another story. What can we do to prevent ourselves from being swept into a similar situation?

Here are some things to consider. We should ask ourselves if we have all the information? Proverbs 18:13 says, "Spouting off before listening to the facts is both shameful and foolish." When we don't do our due diligence before entering the fray, we put ourselves in a position to assume what we say is truth, or we spread rumors that have no substance, or we become a part of a gossip train. Another question we should ponder before taking any action is, "Do I have enough relational equity to offer good counsel?" Someone once said that unsolicited advice is rarely regarded. So many people jump in to make suggestions when they have little or no connection relationally. Lastly, we should ask ourselves the question, "Have I been authorized or do I have enough influence to be a solution instead of a hinderance?" We can impede those with the ability to make restorative decisions, if we presume upon our own position in the relationship or organization. Have you done your fact finding due diligence or are you passing on unreliable second hand information? Do you have sufficient relational equity? Are you positioned to make decisions that can change things? If not, then it's none of your business.

DAILY ESSENTIALS

HERE IS MY QUESTION: Are you in any conflicts that are none of your business?

_____

_____

_____

_____

_____

_____

_____

_____

HERE IS MY CHALLENGE: Work hard to stay out of relational wars.

_____

_____

_____

_____

_____

_____

_____

_____

PRINCIPLES FOR LIFE MANAGEMENT

Daily Essential Eight - BETTER TOGETHER!

I have a picture that depicts the heart and soul of my book, Essentials / Bridging the Gap. Which, by the way, is available at http://bogardgroup.com.

What I love about the picture is the diversity. It portrays four churches, three generations, two nations, three races, four cities, and five husband/wife leadership teams. We were training leaders from several local churches in Michigan. I'm a little prejudiced, but we hit the ball out of the park that day! Why? Each of us brought our individual strengths, which in themselves were outstanding! However, as the day progressed, we realized how much better our individual sessions were because of how they tied into what others taught in their sessions. We were so much better together than if any one of us had the whole day to do the training.

DAILY ESSENTIALS

HERE IS MY QUESTION: Have you ever experienced the synergy of a team?

_____
_____
_____
_____
_____
_____
_____
_____

HERE IS MY CHALLENGE: Write down that experience and make note of the diversity that was present in the individuals that made the team successful.

_____
_____
_____
_____
_____
_____
_____
_____
_____

#dontdolifealone #twoarebetterthanone

#morethanjustaslogan

PRINCIPLES FOR LIFE MANAGEMENT

Daily Essential Nine - LET THE SUNSHINE IN

I am sitting here in some beautiful Michigan fall sunshine! The colors are changing and a gentle breeze is scattering the fallen leaves. It is refreshing. My Beautiful Rose of Texas has been battling COVID for nineteen days with the past ten being extremely miserable. I think about her condition, the conflict in our nation politically, the social unrest, the hate filled racism, the major storms that have hit our coastlines, the uncertainty of it all, and my heart fills with sorrow. Part of me wants to return to my bedroom, turn out the lights, and sleep through it all.

I pause for a moment to look around me. The grass is a deep green, the leaves are brilliant reds, oranges, and yellows, the sky is filled with blue and a few cotton-looking clouds, the air is cool and fresh, and the sun is brilliant. While I sit here and let the sunshine into my soul, I lean into hope. Hope that God will be merciful to our sin-filled nation, hope that humanity will navigate through conflict and find peace, hope that my Beautiful Rose of Texas will recover, and hope that the church will rise to the occasion and offer grace, mercy and love to a messed up world.

The sunshine fills the atmosphere around me with life. It's energy permeates everything I see, touch and smell. The sunshine allows my vision to be clear as it lights up the world where I sit. I must let the sun shine into my soul. I cannot return to the dark and hide. I must lay hold of its amazing grace and live my life in hope! The true sunshine is the Son of God. He came to seek and save the lost. Jesus offered His life as a sacrifice for us all. The day of His resurrection broke the power of darkness and brought eternal life and hope to the world. So I will let the "Son shine" in and put my trust in Him!

DAILY ESSENTIALS

HERE IS MY QUESTION: What do you see around you today?

_____

_____

_____

_____

_____

_____

_____

_____

HERE IS MY CHALLENGE: Look unto Jesus the Author and Finisher of your faith.

_____

_____

_____

_____

_____

_____

_____

_____

_____

PRINCIPLES FOR LIFE MANAGEMENT

Daily Essential Ten - KNOWLEDGE IS POWER

Have you ever been in a situation and did not know what to do? If you only had the right information, you could make an informed decision. Swirling around in your head are different scenarios, the opinions of others and confusion in general. It has been said that knowledge is power and in the midst of chaos having clear direction is an advantage. This is especially true when you are in a spiritual conflict. Paul wrote to the Corinthians to inform them that Satan works to deceive people so they cannot see the truth. By doing so he is able to keep them captive to do his will. The prophet Hosea revealed that God's people were being destroyed because of a lack of knowledge. So, without knowledge the power or ability to succeed is minimized.

Jesus, on the other hand, said, "You will know the truth and the truth shall set you free." [John 8:32] Solomon, likewise, exhorts us to "commit ourselves to instruction and listen carefully to the words of knowledge." [Proverbs 23:12 NLT] You may recall that the Colossians were battling a philosophy called syncretism which was a blend of different religions. Paul's prayers for the Colossians is that they will keep growing in knowledge and understanding; that they will gain complete knowledge of God's will. The knowledge of the truth would keep them from the false religion confronting them. When we face the complexities of life, knowledge empowers us to discern and discover what's true. Knowledge gives us the power to look fear in the face and be confident, because we know that if God is for us then who can be against us. We can be in dire straights financially and not be overwhelmed, because we know our God supplies all of our needs through Christ Jesus our Lord. Satan cannot keep us in depression, because we know the joy of the Lord is our strength. We can be maliciously slandered and not lose our self-esteem because we know that God will vindicate us.

Knowledge is power. It empowers us to live the life that Jesus came to give and that is an abundant life. God asks us to be still and know that He is God. His appeal is for us to reflect on what we know and not what we assume. His call is for us to enter His presence where we know the comfort that He gives, where we understand the protection that He provides, and where we find peace in the storm. We cannot get through this life unscathed, but we can minimize our battle wounds by knowing God's Word and His faithfulness. Knowledge is power, seek it out, respect it, and use it wisely.

DAILY ESSENTIALS

HERE ARE MY QUESTIONS: Where are you losing in life? What knowledge is needed to shift the circumstances in your favor?

_____

_____

_____

_____

_____

_____

_____

_____

HERE IS MY CHALLENGE: Make sure you have a consistent growth plan in place so that you are constantly learning and growing in knowledge.

_____

_____

_____

_____

_____

_____

_____

_____

Daily Essential Eleven - Surprise

Don't you enjoy seeing a fully executed surprise party? The person enters the room completely unaware. The crowd shouts, "SURPRISE!" The unsuspecting recipient is shocked out of their mind! They did not see it coming. The planners pulled it off without a hitch. Fun! Funny! More Fun! Everyone in the room is set in a festive mood.

Life's surprise parties may not come off as well, but life is full of surprises. Maybe a person is called into the boss's office expecting to get an assignment. SURPRISE! They get a promotion. Someone might be going over to a friend's house to hang-out. SURPRISE! Their friend got engaged the night before. A man answers his cell phone wondering why his wife would call in the middle of the day. SURPRISE! They are going to have a baby. Life is full of surprises. Not all have happy endings. Some fill the room with anything but a festive mood.

How we navigate through the surprises of life is important. Sometimes, we maneuver through a bombshell as the supporting cast. We help a friend through a financial hard time, or we celebrate with the friend who received the promotion. We mourn with those who mourn, and we rejoice with those who rejoice. The difficulty comes when we are the subject of change. We receive the news of a loved one's death. A social media post slanders our reputation. Someone calls with a business opportunity, but it requires us to uproot our family. Life's surprises can come from any direction and put unexpected demands on us.

There are several secrets which can assist us as we jockey through the shock. One of those is peace. God promises us peace that overrides the anxiety of the moment. His peacefulness is supernatural and transcends everything we presently understand. Scriptures admonish us to let His peace govern our hearts. We have the promises of God as a sure foundation. Every answer we need is found in His Word. We have the Holy Spirit whose job it is to guide us into truth. The Holy Spirit knows the perfect will of God for our lives and will direct us accordingly.

Most of us have either been surprised recently, or we have one waiting for us in the near future. We don't have to be overwhelmed. We don't have to fear change. We can actually find joy in the surprises of life, good or bad. SURPRISE!

DAILY ESSENTIALS

HERE IS MY QUESTION: How do you handle surprises?

_____

_____

_____

_____

_____

_____

_____

_____

**HERE IS MY CHALLENGE: Enjoy the journey....
Surprise is on the way!**

_____

_____

_____

_____

_____

_____

_____

_____

_____

Daily Essential Twelve - ONE OR ALL?

Have you ever been around someone who was the center of their own universe? We call them narcissistic. You would define these people as self-centered, egotistical, conceited, and in love with themselves. These are not pleasant people to be around. They tend to control their world by being passive aggressive or dominate. They are only about the one, themselves. When they do see the needs of others, they tend to exploit them for their personal end game. You are either cut off or ostracized if you go against them. What drives their narcissism? For many, they have experienced deep relational wounds growing up. Some have suffered severe rejection and shame from a parent, a bully, or an authority figure. They make vows like, "I will never be _____ again," or "No one will ever _____." They are imprisoned by their own brokenness. It takes the power of the Holy Spirit for them to find freedom. Before we are too judgmental toward them, we should consider our own proneness to narcissism.

If we contrast a narcissist with a shepherd, there is a stark difference. Shepherds are concerned about all the sheep in their flock. They will leave the herd in safety to seek out the one lost lamb. Shepherds put their lives on the line to protect the herd from a lion or a bear. Shepherds count their sheep every night to make sure all are safely in the fold. They examine their herd daily for parasites that might bring a disease. They are concerned about the health of every individual sheep. Shepherds are usually strong. They have weathered many storms and remained healthy. They have fought many battles and emerged victorious. When we put this in the context of people, shepherds are those who truly care about all the people in their world. They are humble and caring toward others. They seek to encourage and empower those around them. They desire the best for all, and they are willing to sacrifice themselves to see that happen. Before we would label ourselves an amazing shepherd, we should consider the cost to live a life solely for the well-being of others.

DAILY ESSENTIALS

HERE IS MY QUESTION: How are you responding to the narcissist and the shepherds in your life?

_____

_____

_____

_____

_____

_____

_____

_____

HERE IS MY CHALLENGE: List some ways that you can live more like a shepherd. List some ways that you live like a narcissist. Now write a 21 day commitment to address each list.

_____

_____

_____

_____

_____

_____

_____

_____

DAILY ESSENTIALS

Daily Essential Thirteen - S -T-R-E-T-C-H-O-U-T

Have you ever felt STIFF getting out of bed in the morning? Your back feels like you slept on a rock. Your legs feel like boards. Your neck feels like a flag pole. I felt that this morning. I realized it took me much longer to get the blood flowing and the muscles to relax. Age probably has something to do with it, but reality is that I never stretch. Flexibility evades me and I am less likely to try to beat out a throw to 1st base. I know if I did my hamstring would pop, my calves would knot up, and my Achilles tendon would be destroyed. All because I do not stretch every day…. or year in my case. Research has shown that stretching can help improve flexibility, and, consequently, the range of motion of your joints. Stretching can improve your performance in physical activities, decrease your risk of injuries, give your joints full range of motion, enable muscles to work most effectively, and increase blood flow to the muscle. Stretching takes time and discipline, but the results are worth the effort.

I wonder how many areas of our lives would benefit if we were to s-t-r-e-t-c-h-o-u-t? Take for example relationships. Maybe we were hurt or betrayed in the past and relationally we became stiff as a result. What if we continued to s-t-r-e-t-c-h ourselves relationally anyway? Could it be we remain financially restricted because we are unwilling to s-t-r-e-t-c-h ourselves to learn the discipline of budgeting? How many opportunities have passed us by at work because we were resistant to s-t-r-e-t-c-h ourselves to learn a new skill? There have been dreams and desires that have eluded us because we allowed ourselves to atrophy instead of s-t-r-e-t-c-h. We can waste away in our rigid routines of life, or we can stretch our faith and lean into new adventures.

DAILY ESSENTIALS

HERE IS MY QUESTION: Where is your life fixed, inflexible, and in need of some stretching?

_____

_____

_____

_____

_____

_____

_____

_____

_____

HERE IS MY CHALLENGE: Develop a 21 day plan to address it and expand yourself.

_____

_____

_____

_____

_____

_____

_____

_____

Daily Essential Fourteen - PEOPLE

Our recent family vacation got me to thinking about people. We saw them at the resort. We swam next to them in the lake. We got in line with them. We passed them on the highways. They were everywhere we went. I have jokingly made the statement, "I love Jesus with all my heart, it's some of the people He hangs out with that are the issue." You may feel that way about a co-worker, or a family member, or a boss, or any number of people. Our world is made up of people. We live among them. We work with them. We need them to have families, to make friends, and to build community. People are people and we are one of them.

Stop and consider the two greatest commandments Jesus gave us: 1) Love God with all your heart, soul and mind. 2) Love your neighbor as yourself. Both are focused on people. The first commandment is about us loving God. Our love is to be filled with trust (heart), passion (soul), and commitment (mind). When we love God in this manner, He reveals who we are and what His plan is for our lives. He gives us the capacity to love ourselves and to establish our identity. Our relationship with Him builds the foundation for us to love others. The second commandment is focused on us loving others. We accomplish that from the posture of self-love that we discover when we love God. It's how we love others through the prism of grace, acceptance, transparency, honor, and truth. We have the courage to love because God gave us the gift to love ourselves through the same prism required to love others. Without self-love, we see people through the eyes of suspicion, jealousy, prejudice, pride, and other negative paradigms. Our capacity to love people is therefore diminished because we no longer love ourselves or God.

People are difficult because we live in a fallen world. People are broken. People are wounded. People are selfish. A fallen world leaves people desperately seeking acceptance, approval and affirmation. People want to be known and feel their life matters. People want to be supported and have an opportunity to contribute. People want to be valued and be honored for their uniqueness. People are God's passion! They are on every corner. We see them everyday. When they pass us they tend to visually portray the lyrics of the old Beatles song whose chorus reads: *'All the lonely people, Where do they all come from? All the lonely people, Where do they all belong?"*

DAILY ESSENTIALS

HERE IS MY QUESTION: Who is passing by you?

_____

_____

_____

_____

_____

_____

_____

_____

_____

HERE IS MY CHALLENGE: What if you set aside one day a month and made that day about everyone else in your world and not about you?

_____

_____

_____

_____

_____

_____

_____

_____

_____

_____

PRINCIPLES FOR LIFE MANAGEMENT

Daily Essential Fifteen - NOT WITHOUT A FIGHT!

Are you feeling **overwhelmed**? Does your life seem **hopeless**? Do you feel **locked down**? Are your days filled with **anxiety**? You need to know you are not alone. Others are feeling the same emotions and struggle that you are today. The good news is that **you can get through this moment**. Everything in you may push back against that truth, but you can get through this moment! You may say to yourself, "Everyone else may get through today, but I won't, because my situation is different." You may resolve on the inside that no one has the special conditions of life that you do. You're right in the sense of specifics, but you are wrong in terms of the nature of the fight. So, again, **YOU CAN** make it through this moment! You need to stand and proclaim to everything and everyone coming against you, **"NOT WITHOUT A FIGHT!"**

Think about this for a moment. Two toddlers playing nice in a room full of toys. Everything is going well until one toddler decides he wants the other toddler's toy. The whole atmosphere of the room changes. Where there was joy now there's tension. What was fun is now war. How they were friends has now changed into how they are enemies! The one possessing the toy ultimately says to the other, **"NOT WITHOUT A FIGHT!"**

There is a toddler, metaphorically speaking, that wants your toy. He wants to steal your finances. He is determined to take your peace. He desires to destroy all the relationships in your life. He seeks every opportunity to kill your dreams, crush your spirit, and pulverize your potential. Today is the day you stand up and declare, **"NOT WITHOUT A FIGHT!"**

DAILY ESSENTIALS

HERE IS MY QUESTION: Are you going to cry or are you going to fight?

_____
_____
_____
_____
_____
_____
_____
_____

HERE IS MY CHALLENGE: Don't live another day with excuses! Take it on and FIGHT!

_____
_____
_____
_____
_____
_____
_____
_____

PRINCIPLES FOR LIFE MANAGEMENT

Daily Essential Sixteen - WHAT'S HAPPENING UNDER YOUR NOSE?

Have you ever been in a tense or stressful situation and spout off your frustration? Did you ever say something in an argument that you deeply regretted later? What happens under our noses can get us into some difficult situations if we are not careful. Words have power. Words cut deep. Words can destroy or build up. How did you feel when your father said, "I'm so proud of you?" Maybe he never did, how did you feel never hearing those words? Think about the highest compliment you've ever received and the impact that it had on you. Words can be life-giving or they can plunge us into brokenness.

It's interesting that in order to become a follower of Jesus I have to use my words. What I believe in my heart has to be expressed by the words that I speak. Here are a couple of considerations when we consider what is happening underneath our noses. Take into account that words emerge from the heart. The heart is the place where we process all of life. If we experienced a culture where everyone spoke to each other harshly, then it stands to reason the words that come out of our hearts in seasons of frustration are harsh. What is embedded in our hearts will be the catalyst for the words that we choose to speak, the tone in which we speak them, and the purpose for which we use them. Someone who is jealous might use their words to sabotage the reputation of their competitors. Jealousy in their hearts formed the words they spoke to others.

The difficulty is that our hearts are deceitful because we were born with a nature to sin. The psalmist David said, "I have hidden your word in my heart, so that I won't sin against you." Our hearts have to be reborn by the Spirit of God, renewed by the Word of God, and restored by the Power of God. Lastly, we have to be reminded that our words contain life or death in them. Paul the apostle exhorted us to be swift to hear, but slow to speak. Why? He knew that once we speak we release life or death. Words of death are spoken by a sharp tongue and cutting words that come out of a broken heart. You may have heard the term "hurting people, hurt people." They use their words to gossip, slander, deceive, undermine, manipulate, and control things toward their end game. Their hearts justify their actions because their hearts are evil. Words of life are spoken to restore, to build up, to inspire, to affirm, to heal, and to empower. They flow from hearts that have been healed. We could coin the term "healed people, heal people." They filter their words before they speak, because although their hearts are healed they still carry the scars of brokenness.

Paul said be slow to speak. Life or death are contained in the words that we speak. Choose life-giving words in your marriage, on your social media posts, around your co-workers, among your friends, and whenever the opportunity comes your way.

DAILY ESSENTIALS

HERE IS MY QUESTION: What is happening under your nose?

_____
_____
_____
_____
_____
_____
_____
_____
_____

HERE IS MY CHALLENGE: Change it or Strengthen it.

_____
_____
_____
_____
_____
_____
_____
_____
_____

DAILY ESSENTIALS

Daily Essential Seventeen - WILLING OR NOT

I remember when I was a young boy, maybe ten, I used to go to the public swimming pool every summer. The pool was a great place to be on those hot west Texas summer days. One particular year my goal was to advance to the high diving board. I had mastered the low board, but my friends were all high divers. The day came when I was willing to take the leap. My first climb up those stairs was almost more than I could bear. Once I was at the top, I realized the ladder was the easy part. Now, I had to walk out to the end of a narrow board suspended about sixteen feet above the water and I'm afraid of heights. How long it took me to make the jump I'm not quite sure. I remember my friends yelling for me to jump. I can still hear the life guard's whistle ordering me to jump. I can still recall my mind telling me "not" to jump. Finally, after what seemed like a lifetime, I took the plunge. I surfaced unharmed. I lived through it. That wasn't bad at all. Actually, it was a blast.

My thought for the day centers around the contrast between two perspectives: 1) Your willingness can be a catalyst for your dreams to advance. 2) Your unwillingness can be an obstacle and get in the way of advancing your dreams.
I had to be willing to climb the ladder first. Each step took me higher and closer to one of my greatest trepidations, fear of heights. Once I made it to the top, I faced the issue of the suspended narrow diving board. Again, I had to be willing to walk to the end of the board. Then, the willingness to jump. On the other side of all of it was the thrill of high diving! Had I never taken that journey I would still be a low board diver. My unwillingness to push forward would have been an obstacle to the thrill of high diving. I'm not saying I would have been a failure or a bad person if I had stayed on the low board. I am saying that the opportunity to be a high diver would have passed me bye because of my unwillingness to take on the challenge.

PRINCIPLES FOR LIFE MANAGEMENT

Think about it this way: On the other side of my willingness to forgive is a restored relationship. On the other side of my willingness to be generous a displaced single mom might have a place to be restored. On the other side of my willingness to be uncomfortable may be a person who doesn't look like me, but is ready to accept salvation. We must battle through so many things that want to nullity our willingness; hard heartedness, selfishness, fear, the unknown, past experiences. Being willing is the catalyst for new adventures, new experiences, new relationships, new values, new businesses, new books, new leadership, or new opportunities we might never have dreamed of in our lives. Willing or not… your choice!

DAILY ESSENTIALS

HERE IS MY QUESTION: Will you continue to remain secure on the low board or will you take on the challenge to climb the ladder?

_____
_____
_____
_____
_____
_____
_____
_____
_____

HERE IS MY CHALLENGE: Stop walking under the high dive! Be willing to take it on!

_____
_____
_____
_____
_____
_____
_____
_____
_____

PRINCIPLES FOR LIFE MANAGEMENT

Daily Essential Eighteen - ONE

When I was younger, I used to listen to the song by Three Dog Night called, "One." The lyrics were repetitious, "One is the loneliest number that you'll ever do." I was too young at the time to understand, but the song was actually depressing, especially if you were single. One line says, "It's just no good anymore since you went away." Those words make you feel the heartache of losing someone, the pain of betrayal, and the hurt that you were not enough. You assume the universe stopped the day they walked out the door. Now you are alone to face the world by yourself. One becomes your number and it is a lonely number. Inside a thought emerges that **"one"** will be your number forever. Depression wants to take over. Rejection wants to define you. Hopelessness wants to reign over you.

I remember a moment like that when I was in college. I had been dating a girl for several months. I had actually talked to my mom about how I could know if I had found **"the one."** When we returned from Christmas break, she informed me she was engaged to her old boyfriend. **One became my number.** I was devastated. I had a good friend attempt to comfort me. He said, "there are more fish in the sea." I couldn't see that as a reality at the moment. I was in one of the loneliest periods of my life. However, several weeks later I walked into a restaurant on campus and met the Beautiful Rose of Texas (my wife of forty-five years at this writing).

Broken relationships can put you in a spin faster than you can blink an eye. However, they are not the end of your story. You may have experienced an earth-shattering breakup. A best friend may have betrayed confidence of a serious personal nature. Team members could have turned on you and cost you your job. Your marriage may have just crashed and burned. **Yet, "one" is not your number!**

You will never be a "one" in this life! Why? Because you have *a friend that sticks* closer than a brother, His name is Jesus. Why? Because your heavenly Father promised He would *never leave you* or forsake you! Why? Because you have been placed into His *family forever!*

Lift your head up. Give your heart permission to trust again, love again, and engage again. **One is not your number, refuse to live like it!**

DAILY ESSENTIALS

HERE IS MY QUESTION: Where do you battle with the "one" syndrome?

_____

_____

_____

_____

_____

_____

_____

_____

_____

HERE IS MY CHALLENGE: Show up for someone today and destroy the isolation they might be feeling!

_____

_____

_____

_____

_____

_____

_____

_____

_____

DAILY ESSENTIALS

Daily Essential Nineteen - SOLACE IN THE STORM

Recently in our neighborhood someone has been setting off fireworks almost every night. I am talking about the big ones you would normally see at a festival. It isn't just one or two , it's several intermittently for a couple of hours. I love a good fireworks display, but not every night when we are trying to relax and prepare for bed. When things should be quiet, they are exploding their arsenal. This morning I thought about how life does that to us sometimes. When we are looking for a peaceful reprieve, it can seem like all hell is breaking loose. The silence is shattered by circumstances that are beyond our control. The noise drowns out all sanity and chaos seems to rule the day. How do we find peace? Will there be an end to this situation? Is there any hope?

There is a place where we can find solace in the storm. It is a place of battle, yet it brings comfort. It is filled with aggression, yet it provides tranquility. It is noisy, yet it quiets the tempest. It requires a sacrifice, yet it brings provision. Many pass by it because it seems unreasonable. Others neglect it being persuaded that it only works for some. Yet, I have seen it silence my enemies. I have experienced its overwhelming serenity in the midst of turmoil. It has taken me through many trials and brought me strength when I was weak.

What am I talking about? I am talking about His presence, His word, His promises that I find in a sanctuary of worship. When I declare His praises in the hour of my need, He mobilizes all of heaven to bring me aide. When I lift up a shout of praise in the midst of my battle, He comes to fight alongside me. When I pause to worship in the middle of my anxiety, He pours out His supernatural peace upon me. There is solace in the storm and it is found in the place of worship.

DAILY ESSENTIALS

HERE IS MY QUESTION: How long will you let the noise drown out your peace?

_____

_____

_____

_____

_____

_____

_____

_____

HERE IS MY CHALLENGE: Fortify yourself in worship... right now!

_____

_____

_____

_____

_____

_____

_____

_____

_____

DAILY ESSENTIALS

Daily Essential Twenty - WHEN THE LIGHTS GO OUT

The Beautiful Rose of Texas and I enjoy watching tv. We usually like series that involve crime-fighting and mystery. It is inevitable at some point the swat team, the stormtroopers, or the FBI are going to break into a house full of criminals. Every time they use their little flashlights held up to their guns. Rose knows immediately what's about to come out of my mouth, "Why don't they just turn on the lights?" I'm sure they learned why in the police academy, but I didn't, and it drives me crazy. There is a light switch on the wall that will illuminate the whole room! Yet, they move from room to room flashing this little beam around portions of the place. If I am a criminal, I know right where they are, and where they are coming from. While they are still trying to find me, I see them clearly.

I wonder how many houses we pass by every day that have someone residing in the dark. They are hiding because of their crimes (sins). The exterior of their house appears well kept. From the outside, you cannot see the brokenness that's just inside their front door. There is no evidence that someone is home. Maybe we knock on their door, maybe we don't. It could be, we assume if they are there, they don't want to be bothered. They keep their pain quiet so not to arouse suspicion. Every moment that passes without interruption allows them the opportunity to go deeper into their corruption. They have the lights off on purpose because they fear exposure. So, we pass by. Monday. Tuesday. Week one. Week two. Months roll by. As time passes, we catch glimpses of their activities. Eventually, we know they are living in the shadows. Finally, we go in to investigate.

I often wonder though what miracle is lurking in the shadows? What healing could be ready to spring forth? What relationship is about to blossom? What conversation is waiting on the other side of the locked door? There are miracles in the shadows, hope in the corners, new life waiting to be released. We have the ability to open those amazing opportunities. The simple act of a knock on the door, turning a light on, extending our hands beyond ourselves, allowing ourselves to be a little uncomfortable, or stretching forth and extending who we are to be the light in someone's darkness. Yet this is where we begin to lead beyond our limits, love beyond our conditions, and live with intentionality.

When the lights go out, someone needs to turn them on.

DAILY ESSENTIALS

HERE IS MY QUESTION: Are you aware?

_____

_____

_____

_____

_____

_____

_____

_____

HERE IS MY CHALLENGE: Turn on the lights!

_____

_____

_____

_____

_____

_____

_____

_____

_____

PRINCIPLES FOR LIFE MANAGEMENT

Daily Essential Twenty-one - IT'S A MATTER OF THE HEART

No romantic novel here! This is not a love story! It is an all-out war! It is a matter of the heart! There are several scriptures to consider. Proverbs 4:23 says, "Guard your heart above all else, for it determines the course of your life." Here is what must be understood, **"We have to guard our hearts"**. The heart needs to be protected, and Ephesians 4:18 tells us the why, "Their minds are full of darkness; they wander far from the life *God* gives because they have closed their minds and hardened their hearts against him."

When we let our guard down, we open up ourselves to wander from the life flow of God's spirit and put our hearts at risk of becoming hardened toward God. **What makes a matter of the heart difficult** is found in Jeremiah 17:9, "The human heart is the most deceitful of all things, and desperately wicked. Who really knows how bad it is?" You can not trust your heart. I saw a sign the other day and it read, "Follow Your Heart." That sounds amorous, but it's bad advice. Your heart will lead you astray if you do not defend it. The psalmist prayed, "Let the words of my mouth and the meditation of my heart be acceptable in Your sight, O Lord, my strength and my Redeemer." Why would he pray such a prayer? Maybe the answer is in Proverbs 16:5 "Everyone proud in heart is an abomination to the Lord." Unless our heart has safeguards around it, it will become lifted up and seek to exalt itself in its own self-righteousness.

So, how do we guard our hearts? How do we protect the very place from which our life is directed? How do we manage something that is so important and yet so prone to duplicity? The answer is quite simple, and it comes from a man who was known as, "a man after God's own heart." David writes, "I have hidden your word in my heart, that I might not sin against you." The key to a pure heart, an undefiled heart, an upright heart is to center our hearts in the Word of God. We see it again in Psalms 40:8, "I delight to do Your will O my God, And Your law is written in my heart." His word is a guide for us to make sound decisions. The Bible gives us instructions that will lead us to the abundant lifestyle that Jesus came to give us.

It is a matter of the heart!

DAILY ESSENTIALS

HERE IS MY QUESTION: Are you defending your heart daily?

_____

_____

_____

_____

_____

_____

_____

_____

HERE IS MY CHALLENGE: Look up all the verses you can find in Psalms and Proverbs that deal with the heart. Now personalize them.

_____

_____

_____

_____

_____

_____

_____

_____

DAILY ESSENTIALS

Daily Essential Twenty-two - MY PLEASURE

Have you ever wanted to visit a Chic-fil-a employee's home? Probably not, but think about it. *Wouldn't you like to know* how they respond when someone in their family says, "Thank you?" It is a given when you go to Chic-fil-a's drive-through and complete your order with, thank you, that the answer is, "My Pleasure." We could attribute their conditioned reply to an excellent training program. You might assume that salary, promotions or reviews could be tied to the "my pleasure" comeback. My question isn't what do they do when it's expected on the job, but how they respond in other environments. Is "my pleasure" an institutional conditioning or does it become their lifestyle?

Let's put this into the context of our lives as followers of Jesus. Does our faith look different outside of our Sunday gatherings than it does when we "go to church?" While we are in the "house of God," do we present ourselves **as caring** for the needs of those around us, only to leave and live like the priest and rabbi who pass by the other side beaten humanity? When the blind cry out, "have mercy on me," is **our instinct** like that of Jesus who called him over and healed him? When someone enters our home to inspect **our "my pleasure" reality**, what do they find? Is our faith a job thing trying to earn favor with God, or is it a heart thing that reflects the culture of His Kingdom? Why is it even necessary to have such a dialogue?

Thanks for reading, I'm going to Chic-fil-a! "My Pleasure!"

DAILY ESSENTIALS

HERE IS MY QUESTION: Did you read the last paragraph and think of others or were you leaning in to examine your soul?

_____
_____
_____
_____
_____
_____
_____
_____
_____

HERE IS MY CHALLENGE: Re-read the last paragraph and answer each question without defending or exempting yourself.

_____
_____
_____
_____
_____
_____
_____
_____
_____

Daily Essential Twenty-three - HITTING THE WALL

Walls are barriers. They impede a person from getting to the next place. You either have to go around the wall, jump over the wall, or tear the wall down to continue your journey. Going around delays your arrival time. Jumping over the wall might be impossible depending on its height. Tearing it down could prove difficult if it is very thick.

Walls are obstacles but not impossibilities. When we hit a wall, decisions have to be made. Many times those choices are influenced by our past experiences with similar barriers. Those past episodes can influence the strategy we take to overcome our present roadblock. Here are a couple of things to consider when you hit the wall!

This is not that. You cannot compare your present wall to any of the past. That wall happened last year, involved different people, required specific resources, and is yesterday's history. You may have been wounded in the process. It may have cost you more than you wanted to pay, but this wall is not that wall.

The present will set the future. What is on the other side of the wall is more valuable than what is on this side of the wall. We cannot ignore the wall in front of us. If we walk away from it today, it will still be there when we return tomorrow. It won't go away on its own. We have to take it on. Therefore, we need today's strategy, resources, relationships, and courage. Our destiny is on the other side of this wall, so what we do with it today will determine the course of our future.

There is hope. You can find the tools, the skills, the funding, or the information needed to scale this wall or tear it down. You can recruit people to the cause because the wall has been affecting them as well. You can because it's your mission. You and this wall were destined to meet at this particular time in history. Do not be afraid! Do not be intimidated! Do not shy away! You have what it takes for the breakthrough, so be strong and courageous!

DAILY ESSENTIALS

HERE IS MY QUESTION: Why are you unwilling to take on this wall? Write it down.

_____

_____

_____

_____

_____

_____

_____

_____

HERE IS MY CHALLENGE: Write one sentence that describes what is on the other side of the wall that makes it worth taking on the challenge it presents.

_____

_____

_____

_____

_____

_____

_____

_____

PRINCIPLES FOR LIFE MANAGEMENT

Daily Essential Twenty-four - GIVE HONOR TO WHOM HONOR IS DUE

Today we are focusing our thoughts toward **"Giving Honor."**

Honor is something given as much as it is earned. If I were to tell you all I know about Elbert Pool, you would immediately have respect for him. He is my spiritual father. I would tell you about the countless hours that he spent in prayer for his family, his church, his community, and his country. You would be awed by the stories of his sacrifice to help others in need. I could describe his generosity with his time, his talents, his treasure, and you would be overwhelmed and hold him in high esteem.

Let me pause right here, all of the above are reflections of the man who introduced me to a relationship with Jesus. Elbert, I call him Uncle Elbert, is a man who is due the honor that is bestowed upon him by his family, his congregation, his community, and his friends. However, although he has earned the honor he deserves, he will never taste the fruit of that honor unless someone gives it to him.

Giving honor to whom honor is due is one of the highest acts of respect we afford another person.

When honor is given, it adds validation to the life a person has lived. It lifts up that person's life as an example to emulate. Elbert Pool is such a man. I honor him today before you in hopes that it will inspire you to give honor to whom honor is due to those in your life.

DAILY ESSENTIALS

HERE IS MY QUESTION: Whom do you need to give honor to in your world?

_____
_____
_____
_____
_____
_____
_____
_____
_____

HERE IS MY CHALLENGE: Live your life in a manner that others would want to emulate it.

_____
_____
_____
_____
_____
_____
_____
_____
_____

PRINCIPLES FOR LIFE MANAGEMENT

Daily Essential Twenty-five - OUTTA SIGHT | OUTTA MIND

Forgotten! Disregarded! Overlooked! Ignored! Neglected! Abused!

ARE YOU INCARCERATED? The above terms can cause us to think of those who are in prison. Their lives and their purpose being put on pause while they are behind bars. Imagine the disconnect from life events and the missed opportunities they are experiencing. Consider the isolation, the loneliness, and the shame they have to contend with each day. They are "outta sight and outta mind" on so many levels. However, I wonder how many times we find our own lives incarcerated? We may not be behind iron bars, but we may be captured by sin. We may not be locked away, but we may be enslaved by addictions. We may not be imprisoned, but we may be confined by demonic oppression. We feel... Forgotten! Disregarded! Overlooked! Ignored! Neglected! Abused!

Who are we? Are we White, Black, Hispanic, Asian, Middle Eastern? Are we rich, poor, suburban, inner-city, male, female? Are we politicians, protestors, stockbrokers, business owners, street people? Are we farmers, lawyers, cab drivers, pharmacists, managers, teachers? The truth is we are any of the previously mentioned.

Here is the sad thing. Many times in our captivity we are "outta sight, outta mind" to those around us. They pass us by like the Priest or the Levite did to the man who fell among thieves. They don't see our pain. They fail to stop and ask if they can help. They are oblivious to our cry for help. They won't take the time to pause and inquire about how we came to be in this place. The good Samaritan comes along, who is from a different race, who may or may not be religious, who may or may not be financially stable, but the good Samaritan stops, offers help, and aids us in our time of desperation. We are seen and valued at that moment. We are cared for and nurtured. We no longer feel neglected.

Recently, I heard the story of a young boy who would not lift his head up off his classroom desk. The teacher implored him to look up and pay attention. Several times the teacher scolded him and demanded he raise his head up. Finally, she called for school security. The officer arrived at the classroom door, observed the boy apparently defying the authority of the teacher, with his head still buried in his desk. Unlike the teacher, the officer didn't demand a response from the boy. Instead, he went over to the boy, knelt down, and asked, "Son, why do you have your head down today?" Whispering back to the officer, the young lad said, "my best friend was shot last night in a drive-by shooting." What was "outta sight and outta mind" to the teacher, was now seen and known by everyone in the room. The boy was no longer alone in his pain. He was no longer "outta sight, outta mind."

DAILY ESSENTIALS

HERE IS MY QUESTION: Have you read Mt. 25:31-46 lately?

_____

_____

_____

_____

_____

_____

_____

_____

_____

HERE IS MY CHALLENGE: After reading it again, be a doer and not just a reader!

_____

_____

_____

_____

_____

_____

_____

_____

Daily Essential Twenty-six - IS FREE REALLY FREE

Buy One Get One Free! Join our Loyalty Club and get a "Free" sandwich! Come in for a "Free" demonstration! It's amazing how much is offered to us as free. Free puppies! Free haircuts! Free attracts our attention and makes it seem that there is no obligation on our part. You drive down a street and someone has placed an item by the side of the road that says, "Free." **Is free really free?** Does free have an **unrealized cost** to it? The haircut cost you time to receive it. The puppies cost you money to keep them. The Loyalty Club costs you time and money to earn a free sandwich. The free demonstration costs you time and brain drain to hear or watch it. The get one free cost you the purchase of one you may or may not need. The sidewalk giveaway cost you the time to pick it up and the energy necessary to put it to use in your world. **Is free really free?**

Some would say our American freedom is free, **but it cost** the lives of thousands to acquire it and keep it. Others would say that Christian salvation is free, **but it cost** Jesus Christ his life, and it costs the follower of Jesus the rest of theirs to live it out. Many assume that free speech is free, but there are people on the other end of our speech that might be **paying a price** for what we are saying. Kids look forward to the day they can leave home and be free to do whatever they want, only to find there are things called rent, car insurance, and other **responsibilities**. Is there an underlying cost to what we espouse as free? Does "Free" blind us to the price we ultimately pay? **Is free really free?**

DAILY ESSENTIALS

HERE IS MY QUESTION: What is your story with "free" and have you ever had free really be free?

_____
_____
_____
_____
_____
_____
_____
_____
_____

HERE IS MY CHALLENGE: Think it through before you buy into "Free!"

_____
_____
_____
_____
_____
_____
_____
_____
_____

Daily Essential Twenty-seven - OLD DOG / NEW TRICKS?

My mom is ninety years young at the time of this writing. The amazing thing is that she gets around on the internet, participates in social media, and has an iPhone. She is able to text, send, and receive photos, as well as FaceTime. Recently I even noticed that she was posting on Facebook Live! I would say she answers the old question: Can you teach an old dog new tricks? She would be a resounding yes, you can learn at any age.

The times we are living in are complex. The world has basically been shut down and is struggling to regain the wherewithal to open again. Racism has come to the forefront again, but this time it seems to have an opportunity to be more than just a media blitz. It appears that all races are joining to not only speak against it, but to have the conversations until a real change occurs. Politics is more ruthless and aggressive than I have seen in my lifetime. The loud rhetoric and extremes from both sides almost leave you in a state of paranoia. The messages on every media platform are conflicting, confusing, and condemning. Social media is full of criticism, judgment, and activism from every sphere of thought and belief. Can we continue in this vicious cycle?

I think it's time for us individually and as Christians to learn something new. A new way to love one another. A fresh approach to the debatable things in life. A creative way to honor each other and value the diversity that we bring to the table. We need to advance in the application of our faith and reflect the character of the Christ we follow. It's time we discover some intentional plans of action to impact our world with the gospel. If you will, we need to learn some new "tricks" and stop being classified as "old wineskins" that cannot contain the new wine. I want to learn more, expand my relationships, build new bridges, and see the prayer we pray a reality; "Your kingdom come, Your will be done, on earth as it is in Heaven." I choose to be current with my faith, relevant to the message of hope, and original with my talents and my mission.

DAILY ESSENTIALS

HERE IS MY QUESTION: Are you willing to learn, to change, to grow, to stretch, or are you cool with the status quo of your life?

_____

_____

_____

_____

_____

_____

_____

_____

_____

HERE IS MY CHALLENGE: Describe the places where you know you are entrenched and have difficulty embracing change. Now, make a plan to shift one thing in the next six months.

_____

_____

_____

_____

_____

_____

_____

_____

_____

PRINCIPLES FOR LIFE MANAGEMENT

Daily Essential Twenty-eight - WHAT AM I FOR?

Over the past several days I have asked myself this question. What am I for? I know what I am against... but what am I for?

I am for bridging the gap:
I am for... bridging the gap between white people and black people; the gap between the privileged and the enslaved; the gap between political parties; the gap between the Church of Jesus Christ and the world we live in.

I am for The **First Amendment** that protects freedom of speech, freedom of religion, freedom of assembly, freedom of the press, and right to petition.
I am for every voice having a right to be heard. I am for peaceful protests, marches and demonstrations. I am for justice being administered at every level of society. I am for authorities being held accountable for their actions from the President to local authorities and tribal councils.

I am for the Church.
I am for a Big "C" church that looks like what Jesus came and gave His life for... a church of "every nation and tribe, every tongue and people." I am for a church that welcomes diversity, loves without condition, responds with grace, honors truth, and comforts the hurting and wounded. I am for the increasing number of multi-racial churches where the elders, the staff, and the congregation reflect the diversity of the world around them.

I am for Hope.
I am for the cause that leads us to reconciliation. I am for this generation of young leaders who are willing to enter into a conversation that reflects honesty and vulnerability. I am for the gospel of hope that Jesus died for all... that God so loved the world... that He forgives us our sins and heals our land...

that whosoever will might be saved, delivered, healed, set free, and made whole by the power of His resurrection from the dead.

I am for repentance.
I am for being honest with myself knowing that I have been a perpetrator of racism because of my ignorance and lack of awareness of my own white privilege. I am for asking my black family for forgiveness because my generation did not capitalize on Dr. Martin Luther King's dream. I am for confessing the sins of my forefathers who were a part of groups that persecuted races that did not look like them. I am for turning my heart in my old age to gain a new perspective, to educate myself on words that offend and presumptions that alienate, and to become a better person of our race (the human race).

I am for you.
I am for you to succeed in all God has for you. I am for you to prosper and be sufficiently resourced to fulfill your dreams. I am for you having access to all the opportunities that will advance your ambitions. I am for you.

So, ultimately, I am for 1 Corinthians 13:1-7.... (Read the text) .... **Love never fails!**

DAILY ESSENTIALS

HERE IS MY QUESTION: Have you decided what you are for?

_____
_____
_____
_____
_____
_____
_____
_____
_____

HERE IS MY CHALLENGE: Define It & Stand by It

_____
_____
_____
_____
_____
_____
_____
_____
_____

Daily Essential Twenty-nine - LIFT THE LID

You have probably heard the saying, "God won't put more on you than you can bear!" I have used that expression on countless occasions to encourage someone facing difficulties. It seems to make sense. A good God wouldn't weigh us down with something so heavy that it would keep us from the ability to fulfill our purpose. Or would He?

I saw a friend's Facebook post recently that put a different twist on this. It read: "God does give us more than we can handle because our assignment isn't limited to our capacity." How did we get from phones on a wall or in a phone booth to a cell phone in our hand? Someone had to *lift the lid* on their imagination. They had to see beyond what was and see what could be. They had to *lift the lid* on their leadership. They had to cast vision so that others could see the possibility. They had to *lift the lid* on their pride and invite others to help. The job was too big for them.

Our dreams should be greater than our capacity or we will live in the lowest common denominator of life. We will see God as a rescue from our weakness rather than a resource for our greatness. We have to *lift the lid* on our faith! We have to realize we serve a God who accomplishes more than we could ask or imagine.

Let's lift the lid!

DAILY ESSENTIALS

HERE IS MY QUESTION: What is the phone booth in your life?

_____

_____

_____

_____

_____

_____

_____

_____

HERE IS MY CHALLENGE: What are the possibilities if you lift the lid?

_____

_____

_____

_____

_____

_____

_____

_____

DAILY ESSENTIALS

Daily Essential Thirty - #EMPTYPOCKETS

My son preached a message this weekend that wrecked me. My heart was pierced when he made the statement, "I'm committed to going to heaven with empty pockets!"

The Bible tells us the story of Jesus watching activities in the temple. He observed the people giving financially to the temple treasury. While he watched, there were some wealthy people who came by and gave their gifts. Many around may have been amazed at the amounts they gave. Then we are told that a widow came by and put in two mites (Jesus referred to it as "all her livelihood). The widow seemingly went away with empty pockets while the wealthy people went away having given only a portion of their surplus.

What compelled this woman to take the action that she did? No one in their right mind would demand that she give every bit of her livelihood to the temple. After all, they were not demanding everything from the rich who were there. There was something deep within this woman's soul that inspired her to give all she had and be at peace with it. All we know is that she went away with empty pockets, and they went away without any financial hardships.

My son's message did not mean he wasn't going to take care of his family. You shouldn't assume that he was taking a vow of poverty. However, some do and that's to be respected. He was speaking to a mindset that I believe we see in this widow. It was the same mindset that the Rich Young ruler failed to grasp when Jesus asked him to sell all he had and give it to the poor. It is a mindset that says the Kingdom of God's purposes presuppose our own. I submit that this widow woman and my son both saw and understood the Kingdom of Heaven! The kingdoms of this world have their focus on religion, business, education, the arts, governments, media, and family. People give everything they have in pursuit of success and wealth. Yet, the kingdoms of this world will pass away.

Empty pockets mean that His Kingdom is worth everything I have and more! Therefore, I will use everything I have, my treasures, my talents, my time, and my very life to move His Kingdom forward. I will go to heaven with #emptypockets!

DAILY ESSENTIALS

HERE IS MY QUESTION: What are you bringing to the temple treasury?

_____
_____
_____
_____
_____
_____
_____
_____
_____

HERE IS MY CHALLENGE: Go to heaven with #emptypockets

_____
_____
_____
_____
_____
_____
_____
_____

Daily Essentials

Part Three
Success Principles

DAILY ESSENTIALS

Daily Essential One - ARE YOU WILLING?

Years ago there was an opportunity to invest in a company that sold a certain type of pastry. It seemed like a foolish investment because of the number of units required to sell to make a profit. Today that company has more than 1,500 franchises worldwide with over 161 million in annual sales. The profit margin of a franchise is over $78,000 annually. Do I regret missing the chance to get in on the ground floor? Yes, but I was unwilling to take the risk.

During a lifetime many random things come our way. They could be financial opportunities, or open doors to advance in a profession, or pathways to a better future, but we have to be willing to make the hard choice. Because I was uneducated in business, I missed a golden business venture. Think back over your life and ask yourself where you missed an opening to gain ground. What held you back from making that choice? Why were you unwilling to step into a new beginning?

Many of these enterprises are unexpected occurrences and decisions have to be made in a timely manner. How can we prepare ourselves? We are definitely more willing when we are prepared. I had a coach once say that the pain of preparation will payoff on game day. We cannot wait until game day to prepare. We must get ready now. Sometimes, in the process of our prep work, we don't know what we don't know. Consequently, we need to educate ourselves. Knowledge brings confidence with it. We are more apt to make a hard call when we feel we know what we are doing. Knowledge can also make us overconfident and therefore we need experience. Experience can tell knowledge where to be applied. My father-in-law was a 42-year veteran of an oil company. He was a field maintenance foreman. Every year Corporate would send its brightest young engineers to the field. My father-in-law's hands-on experience would educate these inexperienced engineers on how their drawings really worked or didn't work in real life application.

The will to act is motivated by preparation, education, and experience. We must also bear in mind our will to act can be impeded by failure, fear, and foolishness. These action killers lurk about in uncertainty, ignorance, and laziness. They seek to immobilize our will to risk. They shout to our soul that we cannot succeed, that we have never achieved anything, and that we face certain disaster. These are lies. These are barriers. These must be overcome in order for us to seize the opportunities that come our way. We invite new possibilities when we prepare ourselves, seek the best education and apply the experience we know works.

DAILY ESSENTIALS

HERE IS MY QUESTION: What will strengthen your willingness to be open to new opportunities?

_____
_____
_____
_____
_____
_____
_____
_____
_____

HERE IS MY CHALLENGE: Recall a time you missed a big chance! Now think through how you could have seized the moment had your will to act been strong.

_____
_____
_____
_____
_____
_____
_____
_____
_____

PRINCIPLES FOR LIFE MANAGEMENT

Daily Essential Two - TOMORROW OR TODAY

Have you ever thought about losing weight or maybe starting an exercise program? Here is what I hear myself saying when I'm considering a new regiment, "I'll start on Monday!" **Why?** I want to put the initial pain off as long as possible. Hey, don't judge me!

We fail to realize our actions today set up our success or failure tomorrow. We call it procrastination. Nothing gets done today because we are putting it into tomorrow's agenda. **We miss today's opportunity to advance and move the initiative a step closer to completion.** Here is an example from writing my first book, Essentials / Bridging the Leadership Gap. I would be on a flight to a client, knowing I had two hours I could devote to writing another page or two of the book. What did I do several times? I thought, I will write at the hotel, so I will watch a movie on the plane. Those hours were no longer available... not that you shouldn't watch movies... but what is the true motive?

You may have heard the expression, **"Seize the day!"** We should lean into that more often than not. Today we have the ability to set the foundation or activate a plan that moves us closer to seeing our dream come to pass. I regularly tell my wife, my kids, my friends, my clients, and myself, "Take it a day at a time." Have a great today.... let tomorrow come tomorrow.

DAILY ESSENTIALS

HERE IS MY QUESTION: Why not now? Why wait? Why put it off?

_____

_____

_____

_____

_____

_____

_____

_____

HERE IS MY CHALLENGE: Put it in your calendar, schedule it and do it! Write a sentence. Meet a friend. Recruit a mentor/coach. Buy some tools.

_____

_____

_____

_____

_____

_____

_____

_____

PRINCIPLES FOR LIFE MANAGEMENT

Daily Essential Three - POTENTIAL

You have probably heard the comment numerous times, "They have great potential!" We make that statement full of respect for the talent, charisma, or intelligence an individual possesses. Someone once said that potential is only potential, but for it to be realized potential has to be activated. The graveyards we pass on country roads or on city streets are full of people who never actualized their potential. Today we pass by individuals on sidewalks, work beside co-workers, or live with family that carry great promise, but the question is what will they do with it?

I would propose that you and I both possess amazing possibilities. How do we move our possibilities to realities? What transfers potential into existence? While there are many directives and answers to this dilemma, I want to focus on one aspect: capacity. The lid of potential can be the unwillingness of individuals to increase their competencies, intelligence, proficiencies, and skill sets. Capacity development is a process that involves pressure, endurance, and time. Very few people with potential have overnight success, and some who do have a crash and burn experience.

Potential has to have sustainability to be fully conceived. Endurance is built through the process of challenges and stress. These work together to expand capacity and lay a strong foundation for our potential to mature. Failure to grow the scope of our talent will plunge us into mediocrity. Becoming content with average destroys the initiative to experience what is possible. It is imperative to push through a mediocre mentality in order to acquire the fullness of our potential. It is necessary to break through the ordinary and common, otherwise our potential remains dormant. It is here that we discover opportunities beyond our wildest imaginations.

DAILY ESSENTIALS

Enlarging our capacity increases our confidence to pursue seemingly impossible dreams. We reach new heights and move closer to our maximum potential when we expand, grow, increase, and multiply our capacity.

DAILY ESSENTIALS

HERE IS MY QUESTION: Do you know your potential and can you define it?

_____

_____

_____

_____

_____

_____

_____

_____

_____

HERE IS MY CHALLENGE: List the areas where your capacity is low and devise a plan that allows you to develop and expand your potential.

_____

_____

_____

_____

_____

_____

_____

_____

_____

DAILY ESSENTIALS

Daily Essential Four - TIME FLIES

Have you ever heard yourself saying, "I don't have time" as an explanation of why something won't get accomplished? It is true there are only 24 hours in a day. Every day is filled with demands and desires that will consume time. It stands to reason that time management is a huge challenge. **No one can rewind time!** Once it is lived, it is gone. Time management is an endless war.

We have to steward our time in order to achieve our dreams. Time is one of our greatest resources. I learned about time in the process of writing my first book Essentials / Bridging the Leadership Gap. **This might surprise you.** I found that my challenge with time was not the amount that was available to me. Here is a quote from the book that puts this in perspective, "Being on top of time management means being on top of self-awareness." **We drive the use of our time.** The workload is always there but, we decide how we prioritize it. I realized we are the portal for time consumption.

I've watched this countless numbers of times with the team members on my staff. They give attention to the things they enjoy and put off what they consider menial. I had to navigate time by being self-aware. My book would still be an imagination if I had not recognized the drive and disciplines I had to personally employ. **Time flies!** We capture it and maximize it by being cognizant of our inner being and motivations.

DAILY ESSENTIALS

HERE IS MY QUESTION: Are you aware of how you are wasting your time? (notice how many you's in that ?)

_____
_____
_____
_____
_____
_____
_____
_____
_____
_____

HERE IS MY CHALLENGE: Log your work week hours... . now ask yourself how you influenced the outcome of your time.

_____
_____
_____
_____
_____
_____
_____
_____
_____

DAILY ESSENTIALS

Daily Essential Five - LEAD FROM BEHIND – Part 1

Have you ever been at an amusement park and observed people fighting for the last place in line? Do you ever pull into a bank, drive through on payday, and look for the longest line to pull into? How do you enjoy going into your state's Department of Motor Vehicles and your ticket says you are number 154 in line? Most of us desire to be in the front of the line, or as close to it as possible. We want to lead the way. The same holds true in working with teams. We want to be the CEO, the head coach, the lead role, the ranking officer, the bank president, or the commander in chief. Nothing wrong with wanting those positions. We have to have leaders, entrepreneurs, visionaries, and superiors to point the way. Someone has to be at the front of the line, but to be at the front of the line you have to have a line. You are not a leader unless there are those who follow. You cannot quarterback an offense unless there are teammates to carry out the plays.

Some have defined leadership as influence. Working from that definition, is there any significance to those who follow? Are the only leaders in the organization those who hold titles and sit in the corner office, or do employees on the frontline have an impact upon the company's success? Can teammates affect the outcome of any given play, or does the play caller determine the results? Have supporting actors ever influenced the vote for movie of the year, or is the lead role the only consideration? I think we can all agree there are levels of influence being realized at various levels of any company, team, family, or gathering. The attitude of those in a traffic jam can be impacted by the obnoxious horn honking individual in the middle of the pack. The incentive of a team can be ignited by the chant of their fans. The perspective of an employee can be altered by the gossip at the water cooler. I call this leading from behind.

PRINCIPLES FOR LIFE MANAGEMENT

These influencers may not have a title or be the designated leader, but they are leading where they have connection and sway. They can affect the morale of their team by their negativity, or they can trigger momentum by their support. There is a residual power of influence that filters from leaders to followers which affects the outcome of projects, goals, and success. Therefore, it is imperative for leaders, coaches, parents and leading influencers to possess the ability to cast compelling vision, create a culture of shared values, and empower those who lead from behind. (Tomorrow... How to Lead from Behind Part Two)

DAILY ESSENTIALS

HERE IS MY QUESTION: How are you using your greatest level of influence?

_____

_____

_____

_____

_____

_____

_____

_____

_____

HERE IS MY CHALLENGE: Think about several areas where you lead from behind and list them on paper. Now ask yourself how to best leverage your influence to create the best possible outcomes.

_____

_____

_____

_____

_____

_____

_____

_____

_____

PRINCIPLES FOR LIFE MANAGEMENT

Daily Essential Six - LEAD FROM BEHIND - Part 2

I have a picture of my son and grandson sitting on a bench during a break in football practice. Let me give you the setting for it. Lando is experiencing Texas football for the very first time. His only prior experience has been playing tackle in the front yard with the neighborhood kids. His dad, Reed, is with him on the bench during a break in Lando's very first practice. Here we only have the picture, and we don't know what's being said. The next day after this was taken I asked Reed about the conversation. Some fathers might be challenging their son to do more or to correct this or that. Other men might be berating the boy for lack of effort or demeaning their skills. Still some might be pampering their son, and telling them not to worry about it just do their best. Reed had an experience, that sad to say, few fathers ever recognize. Reed told me that he was almost teary eyed because he realized that Lando was in his element. Besides giving Lando some advice about how to keep from jamming his fingers, Reed spoke to Lando's distinctiveness. Reed wasn't the head coach or even an assistant coach, but during the break in practice he was giving Orland something no coach on the field could give. He was leading from behind the scene, away from the game, and having a significant impact upon his son and ultimately the team.

How do we seize the moments to lead from behind, and how do we lead when the opportunity is available? Like Reed, we have to be able to recognize a moment. Living a self-centered life blinds us from seeing others. If we are unable to see others, and they pass by us unnoticed, then the moment walks by with them. I call it a moment because it is here, and then it's gone.

Becoming cognizant of opportunities to lead from behind must be developed through enlarging our capacity to care about others. When we really see them, we will become aware of our opportunity to influence. At this point, we must know how to engage and seize the moment. For the sake of brevity, let's focus on one thing and that would be authenticity. How authentic are you in this moment? Are you genuinely interested in bettering the situation or the relationship? Can you honestly say that your motivation is void of any self interests? Is there a bona fide desire and commitment to help at all costs? Your ability to maximize a moment of influence will be greatly determined by the authenticity of your motives, your character, and your commitment.

Leading from behind is not about vying for a promotion, pursuit of a feel-good experience, or a chance to gain personal control. Leading from behind is about influencing so the other person is championed, so the person can feel valued, and so the situation can have the best results. Leading from behind is about grass roots moments that produce life-giving ramifications.

DAILY ESSENTIALS

HERE IS MY QUESTION: Can your remember a time when you were the recipient of someone leading behind you?

_____

_____

_____

_____

_____

_____

_____

_____

HERE IS MY CHALLENGE: What needs to change in your life that will make you more aware of the unique moments that come your way?

_____

_____

_____

_____

_____

_____

_____

_____

_____

DAILY ESSENTIALS

Daily Essential Seven - HOW MUCH IS IT WORTH!

Have you been to a theme park like Disney World and stood in line for hours to ride the latest roller coaster? You watch as others are screaming and holding their hands up in the air! The coaster comes flying down the tracks and like a flash it's around the next bend. The sun is hot, the black top is melting your feet, you are thirsty, the line doesn't seem to be moving, you didn't get the fast pass so you are mad at all the people in that line, and to top it off you need to go to the bathroom! Leaving the line is unimaginable. This ride is epic! You are determined to ride it at all costs! You may not ride another ride all day but, you are going to ride this one! Finally you are on the ride! Click, click, click, as it climbs to the highest point. There is no turning back now! Every emotion you have is engaged as you anticipate the thrill of the ride ahead! Then it's over. You stood in line for hours for a one and a half minute ride. **But it was worth it!**
There is a price to be paid for the things we value in life. Think about the security of a home or a position at work. One has a monetary cost while the other costs hours of education and experience. The question that has to be answered for anything we value, small or great, is how much do we think it's worth. The cost has to be determined and then an assessment has to be made are we willing to pay that price. It could be money. Time can be a factor. What are the risks involved? Will there be obstacles to overcome? We may have to adjust our lifestyle. It could involve moving, changing, growing, working, or creating. The bottom line though, **"How much is it worth?"**

Writing this makes me think of you. I believe in you! I think you have something great to offer the world in which you live. I know you think about things other than your normal daily life. You have some moments that you ask yourself, "What if?" Sometimes you lie awake at night and imagine a world where you could do what you desired. I have been there myself. Times when I think there has to be more.

Could it be that these are times where our discontent is trying to awaken us to new possibilities? If so, "How much is it worth?" Will we be willing to stand in line for hours to take the ride? Can we take the heat and survive the difficult conditions? Is it worth it?

DAILY ESSENTIALS

HERE IS MY QUESTION: Do you have a passionate dream or do you have a mediocre wish?

_____
_____
_____
_____
_____
_____
_____
_____
_____

HERE IS MY CHALLENGE: Click, click, click (...roller coaster...) Are you on the ride?

_____
_____
_____
_____
_____
_____
_____
_____
_____

PRINCIPLES FOR LIFE MANAGEMENT

Daily Essential Eight - THE NEXT STEP?

The Beautiful Rose of Texas (my wife) and I sat at lunch with a mid-twenty year old. She referenced her previous work history, told us a little about her family, and then asked questions to determine her future. What's next was looming large for her considering she was completing an internship. I couldn't tell you how many times I've sat across the table from someone wondering about the future. They find themselves in the place where something is ending and they are unsure of what lies ahead. They want to know how to determine their next step. Maybe you are in a similar situation yourself.

I've learned a few things related to "what's next," so let me share a few with you here. 1) We tend to make present decisions more about a destination than a next step. We are at a place of uncertainty, and we want security. We desire to see the final outcome of this transition. The destination might be job security, a perfect marriage, or the ideal place to raise our kids. It is good to have the end objective identified, but we rarely jump from where we are to the utopia we have in mind. The focus at this point should be on the next step. 2) Life seems to be made up of seasons or shifts. A job loss can create a professional shift. A promotion can start a new phase of leadership. A marriage brings new responsibilities and aspirations. Each season presents opportunity for new goals and a need to redefine the end objective. 3) I have discovered that writing a purpose statement for the new season helps. It helps you determine what opportunities are a yes/maybe and which ones are no/never. You should work until you have the purpose defined in ten words or less. 4) Most next steps are discovered through relationships. The adage "it's not what you know, but who you know" applies here. People open doors for people.

DAILY ESSENTIALS

HERE IS MY QUESTION: Have you defined the purpose for your present season?

_____
_____
_____
_____
_____
_____
_____
_____
_____

HERE IS MY CHALLENGE: Read your purpose statement to several people, a friend, a colleague, a relative, or a mentor. Ask them to comment.

_____
_____
_____
_____
_____
_____
_____
_____
_____

PRINCIPLES FOR LIFE MANAGEMENT

Daily Essential Nine - LESS IS ALMOST ALWAYS MORE

My youngest grandson is Cash but we call him Cash Money! This is his first year of baseball. The Beautiful Rose of Texas and I had the pleasure to be at his first practice. You could tell right away with the exception of maybe one or two it was all the player's first practice. I wondered how the coaches were going to handle this bunch.

Their plan was amazing. First, break the kids into three stations: fielding, hitting #1, and hitting #2. Each station had a very simple exercise. Fielding coach would roll the ball to a player who would then attempt to throw it to a coach. Hitting #1 had the player hitting the ball off of a tee (once the coach could get them to face the right direction 😄). The final station, hitting #2, had the coach soft-tossing a ball to a player who would then hit into a net (well that was the plan). The second part of the practice was to teach the boys to run to first base. Practice over. The process was simple and each player learned three things by the time practice was over: fielding, hitting and running to first base. I've watched other practices over the years and even coached some teams. The game is complex on many levels, but the concept of less is more when it comes to baseball holds some merit.

Let me give you one other quick example. Rose and I have sold several homes throughout the years. On one occasion, Rose had a lady to help us stage the home to sell. She immediately began telling Rose to get all the clutter off the shelves, take pictures down, remove all the clutter from closets, take excess furniture to the storage, and so on. Her goal was to give the client an opportunity to see their stuff in the home and also walk through the house and not feel Claustrophobic. Less was more. I wonder what things we could see if life was stripped down a bit?

What about our lives? What about the businesses we run? What about the organizations where we work? Could the less is more principle apply? I've watched young entrepreneurs launch startups. Their product line is filled with offerings or their menu seems to mirror the one you would pick up at Cheesecake Factory. I've watched young couples get married and in the first few months attempt to have what it took their parents years to acquire. You probably have friends whose lives are so busy they say hello to themselves as they are leaving their house.

While contemplating this thought today, less is almost always more, I thought of In-N-Out Burger. Simple. Hamburgers, fries, and a drink that's the menu. I wonder what our lives, my life, would look like if it was just hamburgers, fries, and a drink. Some might say, boring. Others might realize, more time with family, opportunity to rest, ability to stop and smell the roses. Maybe we should be like the great coach Vince Lombardi who focused on the fundamentals of the game and left the complex football scheming to the other professional teams. Lombardi started every training camp by saying, "Gentlemen, this is a football." By the way, Lombardi had a 738 winning percentage. Maybe, just maybe, less is almost always more!

DAILY ESSENTIALS

HERE IS MY QUESTION: Have you ever stopped long enough to consider where there is too much clutter, activity, or complexity in your life?

_____
_____
_____
_____
_____
_____
_____
_____

HERE IS MY CHALLENGE: Simplify.

_____
_____
_____
_____
_____
_____
_____
_____

DAILY ESSENTIALS

Daily Essential Ten - DESIGNER LABELS

Many years ago I joined an organization that required a certain standard for their office dress code. I have to admit it was a little intimidating for this rural country boy. Thankfully, they gave me a clothing allowance and so I inquired where to shop. Here is where I exposed my ignorance when it came to clothes. The stores they recommended were stores I considered to be for the rich and famous. My family had always shopped at local family stores or outlet malls. We never took into consideration what labels the clothes we wore had, we just looked for the sales. I learned a couple of things over the next couple of years. One being that designer labels denote quality, value, styles, and fashion. When a product is given a label, the label identifies the status it will have in culture. Marketers try to capitalize on this by offering knockoff labels or imitations. The label has great influence on the consumer.

We see this in human interaction as well. Most of us had a label of some type given to us when we were kids. I recall some of the chants we did as kids to demean someone who was overweight. It was cruel. There were labels given to me that hurt deeply. I recall one incident where I asked my mom to drop me off several blocks from school because of the car we drove. Why? Because of the "poor kid" label that someone would most surely give me. As well, there have been times that I have been given a title that set me apart. It gave me positive recognition and authority. It said that I was successful and someone to be heard.

The labels we put on a person mark them, if nothing else in our own mind. It influences how we see them, how we interact with them, and how we accept them. The funny thing is that we may be putting a knockoff or imitation label on them. Why, because we don't really know them. We haven't taken any time to enter their world, grasp their culture, understand their life story, or comprehend their struggles. If we did, we might have a different perspective and use a different label.

DAILY ESSENTIALS

HERE IS MY QUESTION: Are you living under a knockoff or imitation label that someone put on you who doesn't even know you?

_____
_____
_____
_____
_____
_____
_____
_____
_____

HERE IS MY CHALLENGE: Find one person that you have labeled and get to know them… seek to discover and understand.

_____
_____
_____
_____
_____
_____
_____
_____
_____

PRINCIPLES FOR LIFE MANAGEMENT

Daily Essential Eleven - REBOUND

Rebound is a term used in basketball. When a shot is put up that misses and hits the rim or backboard, it presents a rebound opportunity. The ball is up for grabs and can be rebounded by either team. Whichever team is able to secure the ball after the missed shot and rebound gains possession. Without possession of the ball a team does not have an opportunity to score and win the game. How true is this in life? Every season of life presents the possibilities for us to shoot at something; it could be a marriage, it could be an education, it could be an investment, or any number of things pertaining to relationships, occupations, or lifestyles. Some of us have higher shooting percentages than others, but no one shoots 100%. So, rebounding is a very important part of our game. All of us have an opportunity to rebound no matter our skill level, our height, or our position. Rebounding provides us the chance to shoot again. It puts the ball in our hands and gives us the possibility to score.

There are a couple of keys to effective rebounding. The first is called blocking out which simply means to position yourself between your opponent and the basket. This enables you to have the first chance to secure the ball. While the ball is in the air, you should be positioning yourself for the rebound otherwise your opponent will block you out instead. Another important key is called timing. You want to be at the peak of your jump when the ball comes off the backboard so you are the first to retrieve it. Position and timing give you the best opportunity to rebound after a missed shot.

So, how can we apply these thoughts to our life? Everyone in life will miss some shots they take. Unless it's our final shot before time expires, we can recover from a missed shot. We can rebound. Our success at rebounding is dependent upon how we position ourselves financially, relationally, emotionally, physically, or spiritually. We must position ourselves to block out the opponents of depression, betrayal, fatigue, and hopelessness. We must seize the opportunity to secure the loose ball. We must be at the right place at the right time. We need to be ready to jump at new possibilities. We need to leap for advancement. We need to grasp the ball and shoot again. The game is not over until the final buzzer. Shoot. Rebound. Shoot again. Rebound. Shoot again!

DAILY ESSENTIALS

HERE IS MY QUESTION: Do you believe in rebounding or just shooting?

_____

_____

_____

_____

_____

_____

_____

_____

HERE IS MY CHALLENGE: Make a list of rebounding opportunities you have presently. Now ask yourself: "Am I in the right position?" "What is the right time to jump?"

_____

_____

_____

_____

_____

_____

_____

_____

_____

Daily Essential Twelve - THE POWER OF AN IDEA

I grew up in a small west Texas town that my friends and I roamed all summer without hesitation. We would be playing baseball on one side of town and a couple hours later be eating at the Dairy Queen on the other. I loved those summers. One scorching hot evening we were walking by one of the town's two *private* swimming pools. That's when my friend had a brilliant idea. "Let's go swimming!" There wasn't any thought that we would be trespassing. None of us considered there might be consequences. We only knew we were extremely hot and the pool offered some relief. A few minutes later we were splashing, diving, and enjoying the cool water. *I'm glad to report no one showed up to arrest us or ban us from the pool for life.*

My point is that ideas move people. Ideas present solutions. An idea can unlock creativity. When the light comes on and an idea comes to mind the way becomes clear. **Ideas are powerful.** We need them if we are going to fulfill our dreams. They become the catalyst that moves us into action. We can build plans around them. They help us assess the resources that are necessary to complete our initiative. Ideas help people see the vision, the mission, and the role they can play. Therefore, it is imperative that we cultivate a process for idea generation.
There is no one size fits all when it comes to creating ideas. Maybe you need a team think tank and a whiteboard while others need a quiet place with no one around. The point is that you have to generate ideas in order to move forward.
One idea can change everything.

DAILY ESSENTIALS

HERE IS MY QUESTION: Do you know how to activate your idea mechanism?

_____

_____

_____

_____

_____

_____

_____

_____

HERE IS MY CHALLENGE: Over the next month try to originate one idea per week for one specific goal. Write each one down. Share each idea with someone who could help you push it forward.

_____

_____

_____

_____

_____

_____

_____

_____

_____

Daily Essential Thirteen - WHEN YOU DON'T KNOW WHAT YOU DON'T KNOW

My father-in-law worked for an oil company for 42 years. He came up through the ranks and started out as a Roustabout. Roustabouts are entry-level manual laborers. He continued to advance until he became a Field Maintenance Foreman. His role as foreman was to oversee pulling units, roustabout crews, and drilling rigs. He also had the privilege of taking fresh engineer graduates from college (book learners) and helping them apply their knowledge to "real oilfield life." These engineers knew what things looked like on paper, but they had never seen "field engineering."

They did not know what they did not know.

We say, "I've read the driver's handbook!" "I've taken the class!" Yeah, but have we driven the car? Have we tested our peripheral vision when parking? Do we understand the thrust of all that horsepower when we press the gas pedal? It's when you get behind the wheel that the classroom becomes an experience.

We don't know what we don't know.

The game changes when you get on the court or on the field of play. Coaches will tell you that you have to get enough reps (repetitive experience) to hone your skills to peak performance.

Someone told me that wisdom is the ability to apply knowledge (acquisition of the facts) to life experiences (the place where problems need to be solved) and see results. It's the connection of our intellectual learning and experiential learning that maximize our capability.

Classes instruct. Coaches train. Experience realizes.

DAILY ESSENTIALS

HERE IS MY QUESTION: Where are the disconnects between what you are learning, and where you are living?

_____
_____
_____
_____
_____
_____
_____
_____
_____

HERE IS MY CHALLENGE: Be sure you are getting your reps!

_____
_____
_____
_____
_____
_____
_____
_____
_____

Daily Essential Fourteen - ARE YOU SURE THERE IS NO "I" IN TEAM?

If you have ever participated in a team sport, your coach probably informed you there is no "I" in team. It is true, if you spell the word team you will never use an I. The coach's point is altogether different than spelling the word team. The idea is that all participants will pull together and offer their individual talents to reach their objective. How many participants make up the team doesn't matter. What matters is that team members collaborate, hold each other accountable, synchronize their efforts, commit to the playbook, and challenge each other to improve.

Herein lies my question: Are you sure there is no "I" in team? I remember coaching a little league team one summer. It seemed all the parents on my team planned simultaneous vacations. We had to have nine players to play. We were sure glad to see number nine show up at the last minute! We were not a team until all the "I"s showed up. Every single teammate is an I. That unique member has a role to play. They are on the team because of a talent they possess. If they fail to perform at their maximum, the team suffers.

You've heard it said that a team is only as strong as its weakest link. That is an I. There is a responsibility every specific member of the team must shoulder. Once that individual disregards or discounts their contribution, the team begins to fray. Think about an offensive lineman in football who fails to make their block. They leave their quarterback or running back exposed. Consider a salesperson who lands a major client only to lose them because of the performance of the service manager. The maximum success of any team requires the ultimate buy-in and commitment of every person on the team.

While it is true that no team should ever spell team with an "I", it is also true that no "I" on the team should ever be overlooked and dismissed.

DAILY ESSENTIALS

HERE IS MY QUESTION: How are you playing your role on the teams to which you belong? (Marriage, family, work, recreational...)

_____
_____
_____
_____
_____
_____
_____
_____
_____

HERE IS MY CHALLENGE: Write down why your role matters on those teams.

_____
_____
_____
_____
_____
_____
_____
_____

PRINCIPLES FOR LIFE MANAGEMENT

Daily Essential Fifteen - KALEIDOSCOPE VISION

Every kid enjoys looking through a Kaleidoscope. They see the different shapes and colors change as they rotate the end cap. Every twist presents a new and colorful experience to the eye of the beholder. However, many people suffer from what is called Kaleidoscope vision. Kaleidoscope vision is a short-lived distortion of vision that causes things to look as if you're peering through a kaleidoscope. It is most often caused by an ocular migraine headache.

While this is a physical condition accompanied by pain and distorted vision, it also parallels a malady that can impact even the healthiest organization. Like a migraine it shows up out of nowhere and creates an alteration in one's perspective. It strikes suddenly and leaves the individual in a state of imbalance. However, unlike Kaleidoscope vision, it can be anything but a short lived experience. Triggers to ocular migraines can include fatigue, skipping a meal, caffeine withdrawal, stress, or certain types of food. Organizational triggers may be caused by disagreements with strategic planning, disunity with a leader or oversight, objections to cultural practices, offense over assignments or tasks, promotions of co-workers, disappointment with compensation, or any number of unrealized expectations.

When these triggers occur, an employee or volunteer can experience Kaleidoscope vision. Where they were once loyal now they are spending discord. They pull back and put a drag on momentum. They want to validate their Kaleidoscope so they pull others to them and create division. They circumvent decisions, they sabotage plans, they complain out loud, and they refuse counsel or correction. It is disheartening to see the impact of Kaleidoscope vision.

Kaleidoscope vision is caused by pain not by purpose.

DAILY ESSENTIALS

HERE IS MY QUESTION: Are you being led by someone with pain or someone with purpose?

_____

_____

_____

_____

_____

_____

_____

_____

_____

HERE IS MY CHALLENGE: Be strong in your purpose and stay away from Kaleidoscope visionaries.

_____

_____

_____

_____

_____

_____

_____

_____

_____

PRINCIPLES FOR LIFE MANAGEMENT

Daily Essential Sixteen - SOMEBODY SAY SOMETHING!

The tension was so thick you could cut it with a knife. The boss was not happy and he wanted answers now! Everybody was looking around the room. Nobody wanted to address the elephant in the room. Silence. After a few more tirades, the meeting was dismissed. No one was willing to navigate the conflict. All the solutions walked out of the room and the issue remained unresolved.

Life is full of stress. It comes at us from all directions. Our dreams are barraged daily with pressures. In my experience, the greatest tensions involve people. Those around us have differing viewpoints and lenses through which they see life. No two humans see everything eye to eye. It makes us better when we are willing to embrace diversity. It's in the clash of two opposing ideas that truth and personal growth can occur, but that only happens in the arena of communication. Someone has to speak up. Someone has to become vulnerable and put their perspective out there. Sure it will be challenged because no one human has all truth, all wisdom, all knowledge, all discernment. That is why we need each other. That is why we must become comfortable with diversity of thought, opposing viewpoints, and dynamic tensions that emerge.

The insecure will never capture the gold found in conflict. Why? Because they either run from it and bury themselves in fear, or they try to kill it to make it go away. Tension requires confidence. It takes confidence to be comfortable in your own skin and speak up. Only the self-assured can hear (listen to, appreciate, value) the opinions of others. The poised and graceful individual will allow for conversations that are uncomfortable. Character flaws get exposed in tension. Broader perspectives can come into view when collaborative dialogue takes place without constraints. Blinders are removed!

Barriers are broken down! Ulterior motives are brought to light! We must be confident. We must search for truth. We must speak up!

DAILY ESSENTIALS

Here is My Question: Are you walking out of the room with answers because you are afraid of the greatness within you?

_____

_____

_____

_____

_____

_____

_____

_____

Here is My Challenge: Gather a group of people in your life from diverse backgrounds and cultures.... have a real conversation.

_____

_____

_____

_____

_____

_____

_____

_____

_____

Daily Essential Seventeen - STUCK IN THE MIDDLE AGAIN

Have you ever had one of those days where find yourself stuck in the middle of a traffic jam? Yeah that day when you had a ton of stuff to do. Maybe today is one of those days. You're not stuck in traffic but your brain is locked down. You need to get movement but you just can't get in sync. I know I have had several days like that and it can be frustrating.

When it comes to your dream, you may have started out strong. Progress seemed to be easy. Everything you needed was there, resources, people, ideas, finances and more. Now you find yourself up against the wall. Stuck in the middle of starting something exciting and anticipating the fulfillment of the mission. What do you do? Here are a couple of tips:

1. Resist trying to control everything. Sometimes in the midst of chaos we discover something incredible. If you are trying to regulate everything, the opportunity may never show up. Take a moment, take a deep breath, and let things ride for a season.
2. Continue to dream. While you are taking your moment, taking your breath, letting things chill, go back to your dream. Re-write it. Imagine what it could look like if there were no obstacles or restrictions. The vision of how the dream will come to pass can take on new perspective. Dream again.
3. Do not compromise. The middle is very uncomfortable. Sometimes it is tempting to find the quickest way out. Here is where your dream gets tested. Don't abandon it. Don't let someone come and take it from you. This belongs to you and the path of least resistance will only weaken the potential of what is in your heart.

DAILY ESSENTIALS

HERE IS MY QUESTION: Where are you stuck?

_____
_____
_____
_____
_____
_____
_____
_____
_____

HERE IS MY CHALLENGE: Describe what it will look like when you get free and list what you will need to move forward. Now go for it!

_____
_____
_____
_____
_____
_____
_____
_____
_____

Daily Essential Eighteen - Dreams Weigh More Than Excuses

Have you ever been around a day-dreamer? People who have a new dream every other week? One day they dream of being an entrepreneur and the next day they are bent on being something else. Their year begins with big hairy audacious goals, but they never complete them. What do they offer up as the reason for these course changes? Day dreamers are full of excuses. Excuses are the easy way out. Excuses are painless because they always put the blame on someone or something else. Day-dreamers are different from visionaries. Visionaries understand that dreams weigh more than excuses. People with vision take on the necessary demands to see their dreams become reality. Ambitions, goals, and objectives carry inherent loads and liabilities that place a high cost on dreams. The true entrepreneurial spirit is willing to take on the burdens of finance, build teams, create systems, and solve problems. Excuses won't cut it. Excuses will inevitably avoid the responsibility. Excuses are for day-dreamers. You either take on all the dream entails, or you kick it to the curb with petty justifications and never accomplish anything. Dreams weigh more than excuses and that is what separates the dreamers from the visionaries.

DAILY ESSENTIALS

HERE IS MY QUESTION(s): Have you tallied your excuses lately? What are they telling you?

_____
_____
_____
_____
_____
_____
_____
_____
_____

HERE IS MY CHALLENGE: Dream Big. Count the Cost. Carry the Weight. Win the Day.

_____
_____
_____
_____
_____
_____
_____
_____

DAILY ESSENTIALS

Daily Essential Nineteen - WHERE IS MY GENIE

Recently, I watched the newest version of the movie Aladdin with my grandsons. It is a movie that has spanned several generations with its humor, music and storyline. Just rubbed the lamp and out comes Genie to give you three wishes. The challenge is to make the best three wishes for the best long-term results.

Many people live their lives looking for a Genie in a bottle, a lottery ticket, or other forms of shortcuts to an easy life. Yet, statistics show us that those who do hit the jackpot are back to their former situation within a short period of time. They never educated themselves to handle their new found wealth. Their friends are unable to offer sound advice, because they lack experience in wealth management themselves. Most of their wishes center around new cars, large homes, luxury items, exotic vacations, and other depreciating expenditures. They have no clue how to sustain their new found riches. I'm not writing as an expert myself, but I would like to offer a few thoughts.

We live life within a set of values good or bad. These values define what we say yes to, and when we say no to something. When a windfall does come our way, then our established values will guide us. For example, a young woman connects with a young man. Their relationship will develop within the boundaries of their values. Secondly, we live in the context of relationships. Those who are closest to us in life greatly impact not only our values, but our perspectives. Perspective is our viewpoint of life which influences our choices. When we have the right relationships in our life, we make the best decisions. Lastly, how we prepare ourselves will greatly determine our success. Life at its best is stressful, but the stress of life can be minimized by the stress of preparation. In other words, how you prepare will be how you perform (I think I had a football coach tell me that).

Whether life brings us unexpected blessings or we have to grind it out, our values, our relationships, and our preparation will bring us the best long-term results.

DAILY ESSENTIALS

HERE IS MY QUESTION: What trajectory is your life on at the moment? Why?

_____
_____
_____
_____
_____
_____
_____
_____
_____

HERE IS MY CHALLENGE: Give yourself an exam in the areas of values, relationships and preparations.

_____
_____
_____
_____
_____
_____
_____
_____

PRINCIPLES FOR LIFE MANAGEMENT

Daily Essential Twenty - A LITTLE CAN GO A LONG WAY

Yesterday I received a box in the mail. I noticed it was from a company that I partner with and do business. When I opened the box there was a short hand written note from one of the co-founders and a water flask with their logo on it. They probably invested twenty minutes of time and less than $10. The value to me was much greater. They took a moment to recognize my engagement with them. They personalized the gift with a handwritten note instead of a pre-printed card with a digital signature. They gave me a gift that I could use. What they received for their seemingly small gift and time was greater buy-in and loyalty from me. They strengthened our relationship and deepened my commitment to continue to do business with them. A little can go a long way when it has a relational component.

Have you ever been feeling under the weather and receive a text from a friend that they are praying for you? It lifts you emotionally. Maybe you have had a season of life when finances were tight. One morning you walk out of your front door and you discover someone has put a sack of groceries on the porch. Your hope for a better day returns. Has there ever been a time when you were giving your best at work. You wondered if anyone even noticed. The next day you notice something on your desk. It's a handwritten note from the CEO and a gift card to your favorite restaurant thanking you for your contribution to the company. You feel appreciated. These little acts of kindness, these small gestures of caring, and these simple investments of time and money make you feel special and valued. They encourage you to endure, to believe, to achieve, to bounce back, and to have hope. These little contributions fuel your soul, lift your spirits, and encourage your dreams.

DAILY ESSENTIALS

HERE IS MY QUESTION: What does today's essential thought implore you to do?

_____
_____
_____
_____
_____
_____
_____
_____

HERE IS MY CHALLENGE: Do that today... not tomorrow.

_____
_____
_____
_____
_____
_____
_____
_____

PRINCIPLES FOR LIFE MANAGEMENT

Daily Essential Twenty-one - IF YOU ARE GOING TO LEAD - LEAD

The other day my wife and I had the grandsons in the car. Everyone was hungry. I made the mistake of asking the boys where they wanted to eat. It would have been nice had they all yelled in unity, "Chic-fil-a!" The next ten minutes were filled will chaos, fighting, and indecision. Why? Because each of them wanted their own way or they didn't want the other to have their way. Finally, I had had enough and said Bobo is choosing and that's it.

Most endeavors we embark upon will have multiple options on how to attain our objective. I think that is what makes visions, missions, and dreams so exciting. Maybe I feel that way because "strategy" is my number one strength in the strength finders matrix. I love discovering the options and resources to attack a project. However, there are always those on the outside that want to tell you how to get things accomplished. Don't get me wrong, I am a strong advocate for having strong team input. I value diversity, I have high regard for feedback, and I invite scrutiny of all plans. At the end of the day, a final decision has to be made and the leader has to make that call. Remember it's your dream, your assignment, your responsibility, and your call.

If you are going to lead…. LEAD!

DAILY ESSENTIALS

HERE IS MY QUESTION: Who is hijacking your mission?

_____
_____
_____
_____
_____
_____
_____
_____
_____

HERE IS MY CHALLENGE: If you are going to lead, lead.

_____
_____
_____
_____
_____
_____
_____
_____

BOGARDGROUP
M I N I S T R I E S

360° Masterplan

The 360° Masterplan is a proven strategy to give you the direction, health and increase you desire. We provide various levels of coaching that include onsite and online assessments to take your organization to the win it deserves.

EXECUTIVE LEVEL (1YR COACHING PLAN)

- 360° Church Health Survey
- 3 Days On-site with Your Leadership
- Full Day of On-site Leadership Evaluation
- 2 Days of Follow-up Either On-site or Over Video
- 10 Monthly Video Coaching Calls

PREMIUM LEVEL (3 MONTH COACHING PLAN)

- 3 Days On-site with Your Leadership
- Full Day of Strategic Plan Evaluation
- 2 Hour Video Conference Coaching with Team Leads
- 3 Monthly Video Coaching Calls

ADDITIONAL CONSULTING OPTIONS

- Personal 1-on-1 Coaching
- In-person or Video Call Coaching
- By Yourself or with Your Spouse

SCHEDULE YOUR FREE CONSULTATION TODAY

BOGARDGROUP.COM

217

FIND OUT MORE AT: bogardgroup.com/book

ABOUT THE AUTHOR

Bobby Bogard has over 45 years of ministry that spans a broad range of specialized areas within church and non-profit organizations. His experience includes 25 years of senior level leadership within mega-church and multi-site environments. Bobby has been a "pastor to pastors" throughout his ministry. His calling is to be a "father to the fatherless". He is passionate about approaching leadership from a generational perspective.

Bobby and his wife, Rose (better known as The Beautiful Rose of Texas), founded The Bogard Group because they believe "Every Leader Matters". The Bogards never want to see a leader or pastor lead alone. They desire to maximize their comprehensive experience to see every leader and organization achieve the passionate mission that compelled them to exist. They believe healthy growing leaders will lead healthy growing churches and organizations which are the hope of the world!

Made in the USA
Las Vegas, NV
20 September 2021